THE

PEASANTRY OF BENGAL

THE PEASANTRY OF BENGAL

BEING

A VIEW OF THEIR CONDITION UNDER THE HINDU,
THE MAHOMEDAN, AND THE ENGLISH RULE,
AND A CONSIDERATION OF THE
MEANS CALCULATED TO
IMPROVE THEIR FUTURE
PROSPECTS.

BY

ROMESH CHUNDER DUTT, B. C. S.

GYAN

Published by

Gyan Publishing House
5, Ansari Road
Daryaganj, New Delhi-110002
Phone: 011-47034999, 9811692060
E-mail: books@gyanbooks.com

Distribution Network
gyanbooks.com
India, USA, Canada, UK, Australia, France

ISBN: 978-81-212-7953-6 (PB)
First Published, 1874

2nd Impression 2023

Printed at: Gyan Press, Delhi.

THE PEASANTRY OF BENGAL
Author: ROMESH CHUNDER DUTT

THE PEASANTRY OF BENGAL

BEING

A VIEW OF THEIR CONDITION UNDER THE HINDU, THE MAHOMEDAN, AND THE ENGLISH RULE, AND A CONSIDERATION OF THE MEANS CALCULATED TO IMPROVE THEIR FUTURE PROSPECTS.

BY

ROMESH CHUNDER DUTT, B.C.S.,

BARRISTER-AT-LAW, MIDDLE TEMPLE.

——— I paint the cot,
As truth will paint it, and as bards will not.
CRABBE.

CALCUTTA:—THACKER, SPINK & CO.,
LONDON:—TRÜBNER & CO.,
Publishers.

1874.

I. C. BOSE & CO., PRINTERS, STANHOPE PRESS, 249, BOW-BAZAR STREET, CALCUTTA.

TO MY YOUNGER BROTHER

ABINASH CHUNDER DUTT.

The following pages

ARE DEDICATED

AS

A TOKEN OF

A BROTHER'S SINCERE AFFECTION.

PREFACE.

MOST of the following chapters previously appeared in the pages of the *Bengal Magazine*, and their republication in the form of a book calls for an explanation, the more specially as they do not pretend to any merit such as would justify their reappearance. The only explanation, however, that is offered, lies in the importance of the subject, as well as in the very painful conviction which the writer has often felt, that the claims of the cultivating classes have somehow been ignored and unrecognized. An attempt therefore to direct the attention of the public to the subject will, it is hoped, be considered pardonable.

The rulers of the country have never been wanting in sympathy for the poorest classes of the people; but a want of a thorough knowledge of the country, as also a recognition of the all-devouring claims of the zemindars have rendered such sympathy to a certain extent ineffectual. Legislating for a foreign people is always a difficult task, but the difficulty in the present instance is aggravated by the total want of enlightened public opinion to help legislation; for public opinion, such as it is in this country, is one-sided and partial, and would oftener mislead than lead in the right direction. In advocating our rights we often betray ourselves sadly wanting in sympathy for the uneducated millions who really constitute the nation. Whoever has carefully examined the proceedings of our associations and the articles in our newspapers must be painfully alive to the truth of this remark. Rights of our educated countrymen to be employed in the higher grades of public service, rights of the leaders of our community to a place in the legislative councils, rights of zemindars to exemption from all land impositions,—these have been frequently advocated and insisted upon with vigour and eloquence;—but the claims of the peasantry to be educated and to be represented, to be freed from the trammels of ignorance and saved from the oppression of zemindars,—such ideas have invariably emanated from our rulers and not from us. While legislation has been busy for the best part of a century in restricting the powers of the zemindars, our press English or Vernacular sees no such necessity,—while legislation for the past several years has been planning mass education, *we* have been calculating the probable loss that such a measure would inflict on high education. And yet high education concerns hardly one man in a thousand, and all that has been written or spoken in its favor,—all that has fired the patriotism of our countrymen and has filled the columns of our newspapers was for the interest and benefit of our man in a thousand,—the claims of the remaining nine hundred and ninety-nine being ignored or forgotten! All honor to the legislation which has disregarded such public opinion and has toiled for the million as well as for the upper ten thousand.

It is not pretended that such a short sketch as this book is, can contain any new facts or any very detailed description of our villages. On the contrary there is nothing in this book which is not known to the ordinary reader, or which may not be learnt by a few years' residence in the mofussil. We are not aware, however, that the measures of reform, pointed out in the following pages, were ever advocated before, and it is for these that the book ventures to claim a passing notice. We are aware we have been treading on very delicate grounds in advocating such measures. It is an unfortunate fact,—and we write this in shame and sorrow,—that the welfare of the country is identified by our educated countrymen with the interests of the zemindars. Patriotism is another name for the advocacy of zemindars' rights and interests, and a word spoken in favor of the claims of the cultivators is regarded and branded as a certain sign of denationalization. It is not hoped that such public opinion will be at all shaken by anything we may urge; but if there be any *one* of our country-men who after a perusal of the following pages would rise with a wholesome doubt as to the soundness of the above mentioned views entertained by our influential newspapers, our effort has not been made in vain. To such we would urge that what we have written has proceeded solely from strong, earnest and painful convictions,—that if we have said anything wrong we are open to correction,—that if we have said anything unpleasant to any party a stern sense of duty could alone have induced us to do so.

On the other hand there are some among our countrymen, specially among the rising generation, who declaim against the zemindari system as such, and would probably advocate the introduction of some other system. We may declare once for all that we do not entertain such views, and have no sympathy with such thinkers. Considered in the abstract, the system of Peasant Proprietors may deserve the high enconiums bestowed on it by Sismondi, Mill and other political economists,—but it is a question entirely different, as to whether such a system would suit the habits of people and conditions of life as existing in Bengal. The introduction of such a system,—did even the Permanent Settlement allow of such a thing,—would be the exchange of a state of things whose defects we know from the experience of a century, and can remedy, for another full of uncertain evils, which may possibly prove entirely unsuited to the country. But there is another and probably a yet stronger reason why the zemindari system should not be demolished. It has been well remarked that, we are not made of rocks that the things which connect themselves round our habits and hearts can be removed like lichen, sea weed or tangle without our feeling the loss. Bengal has accepted the zemindari system during long centuries, our habits and thoughts have clung around that institution, our traditions and feelings are closely interwoven with it. The institution has become a part and parcel of our society, and to wring it away would be to convulse society at a time of profound peace. Opportunities do occur in the history of nations, and have occurred in that of Bengal, when society is disorganized and convulsed, and old institutions may be altered. But those who, in these times of peace, advocate the abolition of the most ancient and firmly established institution of the country by a stroke of legislation, have not sufficiently considered the probable consequences. It is, no doubt, a fact, apparent to every one except such as choose to close their eyes at it, that in *some* estates, especially in petty zemindaries and unprofitable Patni holdings, Mathote is still freely collected to a fearful extent, making, to our certain knowledge, the amount payable sometimes double of what is legally due as rent,—that in *most* zemindaries Mathote is still freely collected,—that in *all* zemindaries, probably much more, than is legally due, is collected either by the zemindars themselves or by their agents as their special allowances on special occasions,—that zemindars still possess to an indefinite extent the power to oppress, harass and ruin their ryots in a variety of ways against which the law affords no redress, and that therefore in most places ryots are still held in a sort of moral servitude, and comply, without thinking of resistance, with the most unjust demands and orders of their masters. Such uncertain and even increasing exactions, and such moral servitude make it simply impossible for ryots to save anything, or to learn to be prudent, provident, thinking beings, or better their condition; and we have therefore in the following pages advocated the introduction of permanent restraints on the zemindars' powers. But our views on the subject extend no further.

In conclusion we have only to remark that in the following pages we have had several occasions to dwell at length on what we have considered to be mistakes in English legislation in India. Kind friends have pointed out that it is not for a government officer to point out such mistakes. Our thanks are due to their intention, but to their reasoning we have but one answer to make. We feel confident that the British Government is striving honestly for the good of the people, and we also feel confident that the humble suggestions we have made with the self same object cannot therefore be unacceptable. We could not give a stronger proof of our confidence in the good faith on the part of the British Government than by venturing to point out its mistakes where such exist.

R. C. DUTT.

CALCUTTA:
October, 1874.

CONTENTS.

THE

PEASANTRY OF BENGAL.

CHAPTER I.

General Remarks.

'Tis the clime of the East, 'tis the land of the Sun.

Byron.

We purpose in the following pages to consider the present and past condition as well as the future prospects of the Peasantry of Bengal. By Bengal we do not mean the entire province under the Lieutenant-Governor of Bengal, but only that portion of it in which the Bengali is spoken as the native tongue. There are many essential differences in manners, customs and habits of living which distinguish the Bengali peasant from the peasantry of Behar, Chota Nagpur, Orissa and Assam, and, as our acquaintance with the people of these provinces is slight, we shall confine our remarks to those places only which are inhabited by the Bengali properly so called.

The country inhabited by this race may be described as one immense rice-field, stretching from the hills of Nagpur on the west to the confines of Burma on the east, and from the foot of the Himalayas near Darjeeling to the Bay. The soil is alluvial, and the country is intersected by a network of innumerable rivers affording splendid facilities to trade.

There are, however, some varieties in this apparently uniform rice-producing province. The province may be conveniently divided into the Western, the Southern, the Eastern and the Northern Divisions. The *Western Division* may be roughly taken to be the portion of the country lying to the west of the Hugli, known as the Burdwan Division. The *Southern Division* includes the territories between the Hugli and the Horinghotta known as the Presidency Division. The *Eastern Division* may be taken to include the entire territory to the east of the Brahmaputra and the Horinghotta, and includes the Dacca and Chittagong Divisions. The *Northern Division* lies to the north of the Brahmaputra and the Ganges, and includes the Rajshahi and Cuch-Behar Divisions.

Commencing with the *Western Division*, there is to the extreme west a narrow strip of land which forms the boundary line, as it were, between the high hills and plateau of Chota Nagpur and the low alluvial soil of Bengal. This small strip of land has a comparatively high elevation; summer in this place is excessively hot, and the enervating dampness and moisture which characterize the climate of Bengal are wanting here. The people too of this strip are inferior in civilization to those of the other parts of Bengal, and indeed consist mainly of semi Hinduized aborigines. Turning eastward we at once come to the enervating damp climate and alluvial soil of Bengal Proper. The Damoodar, the Darkeshwar and other rivers, annually overflow their banks and deluge a portion of the Burdwan Division. The banks of the Darkeshwar, however, in the present days are protected by strong embankments, and attempts were made in a similar manner to save the country along the Damoodar. Such attempts, however, have now been given up and the embankments on the right bank abandoned, while those on the left are maintained. The effect is, that in the rainy season the Damoodar overflows its right banks and inundates a strip of country to its west about 5 miles in breadth, and a traveller who has to journey to the west of the Damoodar in this season sees before him a shallow and rapid stream, several miles in breadth, from which project houses and trees dotting the vast expanse of water.

The Division of Burdwan was at one time the part of Bengal the most exposed to the incursions of the Mahrattas and other predatory hordes. A century of peace, however, under the British rule, coupled with the brisk trade in and about Calcutta, made these provinces among the most flourishing in Bengal; and travellers who went through the country a few years back gave glowing accounts of the populous villages, careful cultivation and industrious population which marked the Division of Burdwan. A few years' epidemic, however, has completely changed the aspect of things. Villages have been deserted or almost deserted, cultivated fields are turning into jungles, and a fever-stricken population meets the eye of the traveller in all parts of the country.

Passing further westward, we come to the healthy and flourishing districts of the *Southern Division* known as the Presidency Division. This division is something like a triangle in shape, the Hugli, the Horinghotta and the Bay forming its three sides. Innumerable branches of rivers issue from the Hugli and the Horinghotta and intersect the country in every conceivable direction before falling into the Bay. In the rainy season some of these small rivers overflow their banks and inundate the intermediate strips of land. The country is a level alluvial plain, and the climate, as all over Bengal, is moist. The northern portion of this division is raised and exceedingly fertile, the southern part consists of the Sunderbuns,—once, we have reasons to suppose, a populous country with fair towns and villages,—but now an untenanted wilderness and a home of the tiger and the rhinoceros. It is just on the borders of the Sunderbuns,—in a strip of country forming the boundary line between the high lands to the north and the unsurveyed wilderness to the south—that the Bádá, the great granary of Bengal, is situated. Rice grows plentifully all over Bengal, but nowhere in such abundance as in this narrow, swampy, jungly strip. The Amon harvest here is so exuberant that the owners of the lands can never hope to reap the crops unaided, and annually therefore hundreds of thousands of laborers swarm to the Bádá from all parts of Bengal, find employment there in the reaping season, and return home after two or three months with a portion of the dhan reaped as their wages. Numerous huge boats, too, come to the Bádá at the winter season, and loaded with dhan proceed through the numerous channels, rivers and khals that intersect the country, to rice marts in the north. There the rice is unloaded and sold, and thus the whole of Bengal receives annual supplies from this great granary in the south.

This great rice-producing tract, however, is very sparsely populated,—a fact sufficiently explained by the fact that the bulk of the cultivators are non-resident, having their homes elsewhere, and tilling their Sunderbun lands by hired labor. "While a great deal of cultivation in the more remote parts of the Sunderbuns follows this method, there are in the nearer parts large settlements of ryots who dwell permanently near the land they have under cultivation . . . .
There is another thing to be noticed with reference to the dwellers in these regions, that they do not tend as in other places to group themselves into villages. Probably this is one result of their having holdings so large that it is most convenient to live near them. But whatever the cause, many of the village names on the map represent no sites of villages, as we usually understand a village, but represent great seas of waving paddy

with homesteads dotted over them where families live apparently in perfect seclusion."*

The *Eastern Division*, including the Divisions of Dacca and Chittagong, presents some characteristic features and may appropriately be called the Division of inundations. The greater part of this Division is of alluvial formation. The great body of water of the Brahmaputra which used to go through the Megna before, now meets the Padma at Goalundo through what is called the Jumna river. Lower down, the Surma, which rises in the western mountains, joins the combined waters of the Brahmaputra and the Padma (Ganges) at the southern point of the Dacca District. The combined waters present in the rainy season the appearance of a vast sea. "At this season of the year almost the whole of Eastern Bengal is inundated. The eye at such a time wanders over a vast expanse of water broken only here and there by artificially raised village sites which stand out against the horizon like so many islands. Yet all this country is most densely populated and may almost be designated the granary of Bengal."†

The Southern portion of Bakergunj forms a part of the Sunderbuns, but the central portion of this district as well as the whole districts of Dacca and Faridpur are among the most densely peopled places in Bengal. The district of Backergunj is so intersected with rivers

---

* Westland's Jessore.

† Beverley's Census Report.

that communication is impracticable except by rivers. A large portion of this district, as well as Faridpur and some other districts, are, as a matter of course, inundated in the rainy season. The splendid paddy, however, of these districts rises with the rising water, cattle and men are collected in the villages which are usually situated on high sites, and locomation is possible only by boats shooting across this vast expanse of shallow water covered with a forest of exuberant paddy. This paddy gets ripe in winter, and is then cut and exported to other districts, and the *Bálám* rice of Backergunj is consumed by the higher castes all over Bengal.

To the extreme east or rather south-east lie the districts of Chittagong and Tipperah. By far the largest portions of these districts known as the Hill States or Hill Tracts are uninhabited, or inhabited only by a small number of naked barbarians living in the midst of primeval forests and woods. The southern part of Chittagong again is inhabited by Mughs, "who fled from Araccan when it was conquered by the Burmese at the close of the last century. In 1824 the English took Araccan, and the immigration of the Mughs ceased; in the present day the tide of emigration flows in the opposite direction, and large numbers now leave Chittagong to till the rice-fields of British Burmah."*

Lastly, we come to the *Northern Division* which includes the Rajshahi and Cooch-Behar Divisions. As in every other

* Beverley's Census Report.

part of Bengal the soil is alluvial and forms one extensive rice plain. The districts along the Ganges and the Brahmaputra,—*viz*, Cooch-Behar, Rungpur, Bogra, Pubna, Rajshahi and Moorshedabad, are the most thickly populated,—Pubna and Rungpur being among the most densely populated districts in all Bengal. The Padma and the Brahmaputra, but specially the former, become excessively strong in the rainy season and overflow their banks for miles together, and often sweep away entire villages in their imperious wrath. There is, however, no such inundation of entire districts as in Eastern Bengal, though large morasses are to be found all over this division.

From the natural features of the country we turn to the people. The masses of the people naturally divide themselves into two large communities, *viz*, the Hindu and the Mahommedan. The Hindu population forms 50·1 per cent, and the Mahommedan 48·8 per cent of the entire population,—not of Bengal,—but of the territories under review; the remaining small fraction comprising Buddhists, Christians, &c. The proportion of the Mahommedan population is much smaller in Behar, Chota Nagpur, Orissa and Assam, than in the districts under consideration. We do not know if it is very complimentary to our nation that they have always been but too ready to embrace the manners, and when necessary the religion, of the governing race. The tall, and somewhat thick-skulled peasantry of Behar clung to their own religion, though they were not far from the capital and seat of the Moslem Empire; but the Bengali changed his religion and manners fast enough till half the population turned Mahommedans. Nor is it difficult to discover the sort of advantages that they hoped to gain by this change of religion. The Hindu religion with its baneful and harassing caste system has always been oppressive to those who, by the mere accident of birth, happened to belong to the lower castes. The Moslem conquerors came and proclaimed the equality of men, and the most despised of the human race had only to embrace the new religion, and they would be on a footing of equality with their higher caste brethren,—perhaps be superior to them by belonging to the ruling race. If the history of the *people* be ever correctly written it will be found that it was the lower caste people who mostly embraced the religion of the Prophet. Large swampy districts in the east like Faridpur, Backergunj and Dacca, which at one time probably were mostly inhabited by low caste Hindus, now teem with Mahommedan population; and the resemblance which these Mahommedans bear to the Hindus in every respect except religion, and indeed sometimes in religious matters too, leave no doubt whatever of the fact that they are the descendants not of the conquering Mahommedans but of the proselytized Hindus.

We cannot help making a passing remark here about a similar change observable at the present day. The

English Government manifests no partiality for those who embrace the religion of the governing race, and so very few of our couutrymen have embraced the Christian religion. But the present Government does shower favor on those who learn the English language, acquire English sentiments and feelings, and imbibe English opinions in social and other matters. The people of Bengal, as distinguished from those of Behar, Orissa &c., have not been slow to perceive this, and have fast adopted the means of improvement afforded by our Government. The phenomenon of an Anglicised Hindu is to be found only in Bengal. In so far as the conversion in thought and ideas is sincere, it is certainly productive of good,—but often the appearance of liberalism is put on to prosper in the world, or win the respect of the governing race, and then the thing is downright hypocrisy. But this by the bye.

We have said the Hindus and Mahommedans are about equal in number in Bengal Proper. Taking into consideration the fact that the Hindus constitute by far the majority of those who serve Government or occupy the higher ranks of society, we are driven to the conclusion that among the peasantry the Mahommedans are probably larger in number than the Hindus. The distribution again of the Mahommedans varies in different districts. Generally speaking, as we proceed from the west to the east, the proportion of the Mahommedans to the total population increases. Thus, in the extreme western districts of Midnapur and Bankura, Mahommedans form less than 15 per cent of the entire population. In Hugli, Burdwan and Beerbhoom, they make less than 30 per cent, and in the 24-Pergunnahs they are less than 45 per cent of the total population. Further east, in the districts of Jessore, Faridpur, Backergunj, Dacca and Mymensing, we find the Mahommedans numbering at between 55 and 70 per cent of the total population, while in the extreme eastern districts of Noakhally and Chittagong (as well as in two other districts in Bengal, *i. e.* Rajshahi and Bogra) the proportion increases to over 70 per cent.

It is a very widespread error among our countrymen to suppose that the Hindu religion does not proselytize. On the contrary, ever since the Aryans came into Bengal it has been a main object with them to proselytize the aborigines, and large numbers of the latter have now entered into the ranks of Hinduism, but forming separate castes of their own, as Haris, Domes &c. Dr. Hunter starts a very interesting question,* *viz.*, what proportion of the total population of Bengal are Hinduized aborigines. To this question he gives a very imperfect answer. In one place he seems to suppose that all names having at their end the word *Dás* indicate aboriginal stock. This supposition, however, will not hold water; for all people of the superior castes, such as the Kayasthas, the Vaidyas &c., write *Dás* after their names; and a Dutt or a Gupta

* In his Annals of Rural Bengal.

writing his name in Bengali would write it as *Dás Dutt* and *Dás Gupta.* In the same way the *Kaivartas* are all *Dases,* while people of very inferior castes, those who are apparently descended from the aborignial stock, do not write *Dás* at the eud of their names.

Out of a total population of nearly 37 millions of Bengal Proper Mr. Beverley reckons the aborigines (Sonthals, Garos &c.,) at nearly 4,00,000 and the Hinduized aborigines at a little over 5 millions. Under this last head he includes such people as the Bagdi, the Buna, the Chamar and the Muchi, the Chandal, the Dome and the Hari, the Kaora, the Mal, the Mehtar and many other tribes. Though all these are reckoned as Hindus now, any one, who has carefully observed their peculiar modes of living in our villages, would have no difficulty in setting them down as descended from the aboriginal stock. In their habits they present a marked contrast to the Aryans who, even in the worst circumstances, are noted for their cleanliness of living; and some vices such as intoxication they share with the aborigines who are not yet Hinduized.

Brahmans and Kayasthas are about equal in number, being over one million each. Of Vaidyas there are only 68 thousands, and including the Bhat and the Chatri we have altogether about two and a half millions of people of the superior castes. We think we can safely set it down that these are of purely Aryan origin. The termination *Dás* is very easily explained. When the Brahmans emigrated to Bengal with other Aryans of inferior castes they found themselves opposed to the aborigines of the country who naturally enough questioned the superiority and the right of conquest of the invaders. In the wars that followed, therefore, they had their Aryan followers to serve under them who were the *Dáses* and the aborigines to fight with who were the *foes.* This supposition is quite natural, and if it required any confirmation, such confirmation would be received from the numerous traditions of the country about the Aryan origin of the Kayasthas and Vaidyas as also about the immigration into Bengal of those castes along with the Brahmans from the north-west.

The high caste Mahommedans, those who may be supposed to have descended from the conquerors of Bengal and not from convert Hindus, form a very small number. The Pathans, Moghuls, Syuds, Shekhs and Jolahs amount to scarcely half a million. These of course do not belong to the aboriginal stock.

Deducting then half a million aborigines, five million Hinduized aborigines, two and a half million high caste Hindus and half a million high caste Mahommedans from the total of nearly 37 millions, we have about 28 millions still to account for. The question arises, then, have these 28 millions descended from the aboriginal stock? Out of these 28 millions, 17 millions are Mahommedans (descended very probably from Hindu converts of olden times), and the remaining 11 millions are Hindus, of whom 2 millions are Kaibartas and the other 9 millions consist of a variety of Hindu castes, none amounting to a million, and only the Goalas and Sadgopes amounting to over half a million each. Are these 28 millions Hinduized and Mahommedanized aborigines? This question does not admit of a definite reply. It is impossible, however, to suppose that the conquering Aryans should have swept away from the face of the country the cultivators of the soil, and should have taken up that menial work themselves. Neither the Mahommedans nor any other set of conquerors have ever done so. The Hindu conquerors too were never bloodthirsty or cruel; and at the time when Bengal was conquered, their first zeal of conquest and love of enterprize had decreased, and the wave of their conquest had already spread over the whole of Western and Northern India. All these reasons lead us to suppose that the Aryan conquerors of Bengal after causing their religion to be widely spread through the land did not and could not exterminate the aboriginal tillers of the soil. It stands to reason to suppose that, while the brave and fierce aborigines retired to the wilds and fastnesses of Bengal, the weaker population accepted the religion of their conquerors and remained, as they were before, the cultivators of the soil. Centuries rolled on, and those fierce tribes too gradually became reconciled with the humane treatment of the conquerors, or were tempted into the conquered territories by the greater security of life and property there available, or by the flourishing state of cultivation and the arts of peace there prevailing, and were thus gradually Hinduized. The Bagdis and Haris will be, centuries hence, completely Hindus in their habits and manners; and who can question but that the Goalas and Kaibartas might at one time have been what the Bagdis and Haris evidently were, *viz.*, aborigines? We are therefore probably not far from the truth if we conclude that the 28 millions of Bengal Proper spoken of before (if not Hinduized aborigines) have a large proportion of aboriginal blood in their veins.

We have said before that we intend to speak only of those provinces in which the Bengali tongue is spoken. These include what are known as the Presidency, the Burdwan, the Rajshahi and the Dacca divisions, as well as the smaller divisions of Cuch Behar and Chittagong.

These six divisions comprise 27 districts and an area of 94,537 square miles and a total population of nearly 37 millions according to the census taken in 1872.* The density of the population varies very much within these districts. There are desolate hill tracts which own no human inhabitants at all, or own but few. The Chittagong Hill Tracts and the Hill Tipperah, for instance, shew an average of 9 or 10 inhabitants to the square mile. Then come in hilly and barren districts like

* The total area of the provinces under the Lieutenant-Governor of Bengal is 248,231 square miles, and the total population nearly 67 millions.

Darjeeling, Jalpaiguri and Cachar, which shew an average of only a hundred or a hundred and fifty persons to the square mile. Outlying districts like Sylhet and Mymensing, Dinajpore and Maldah, shew on an average between three and four hundred persons to the square mile. The south-eastern districts of Backergunj, Chittagong and Noakhally as well as some other districts, shew a population of between four and five hundred persons; while most of the old districts like Burdwan and Birbhum, Nuddea and Jessore, Rajshahi and Murshedabad, shew an average of between five and six hundred souls to the square mile. Leaving aside large towns and their neighbourhood (24 Parganas and Hughli) this proportion is only exceeded in four districts, *viz* Rungpore and Pubna, Dacca and Faridpore, the last mentioned place being the most populous in the country and containing no less than 677 persons to the square mile.

It is not however of the entire population of 37 millions that we intend to speak in the future chapters. The village population, the peasantry, is our subject. What is their aggregate number? General statement VI of the Census Report shews that out of a *male* population of over 18 millions, over 6½ millions are children. Of the remaining 11½ millions over 6¼ millions are described as actual cultivators of the soil. From this we may conclude that out of a *total* population of 37 millions including women and children, we may put down 20 millions as belonging to the cultivating classes. The proportion of the peasantry who are not actual cultivators is not very large, and we may take them at a round number of 5 millions. It is of these 25 millions then,—these two-thirds of the entire population of the districts aforesaid—that we shall speak in the future chapters.

CHAPTER II.

The Bengal Ryot under the Hindu and Mahommedan Rule.

The man of wealth and pride
Takes up a space that many poor supplied.
The robe that wraps his limbs in silken sloth
Has robbed the neighb'ring fields of half their growth.

Goldsmith.

It is not possible in the present day to correctly ascertain the condition of the Peasantry of Bengal under the Hindu princes of the country. No annals of those times have been left to us, and the labors of our antiquarians are directed to the elucidation of the narrative of kings and princes, and throw no light on the condition of the people. Probably, however, we shall not be far from the truth, if we assume that the condition of the Bengal peasantry under Hindu kings was about the same as that of the peasantry of other parts of India in ancient times. Something too we might venture to deduce from the known principles which pervade all oriental governments.

The ancient literature of India tells us that the king claimed a sixth of the produce of land as his due. How this was collected, or what machinery was employed for the transmission of this revenue to the imperial treasury, we do not know. There are some reasons to believe that the collection was made in kind, and judging from what has been the immemorial practice in India, we may be sure that favored individuals were placed in charge of small districts for the collection of this revenue. In all oriental governments such persons have possessed absolute power within their respective jurisdiction, have invariably extorted from the cultivator more than is their due, have sent to the imperial treasury often less, and sometimes more than what is due to the throne, according as its occupier might be imbecile or vigorous in his administration. This is the simplest method of collection of revenue which suggests itself to a civilized people, and the Hindus, however rich in their literature and philosophy, carried few of the practical arts of life to perfection, and least of all the art of government.

Our supposition that such was the system of revenue collection under the Hindu kings of Bengal, seems to be confirmed by the state of things that we find prevailing under the earliest Mahommedan conquerors of Bengal. We find the zemindari system to be a *fait accompli* and a sort of permanent institution of the land under the earliest Mahommedan rulers,—and this could scarcely have been the case unless the same system had prevailed also in previous times. All *a priori* arguments based on the peculiar characteristics of the people of Bengal would also lead to the same conclusion. With the bold and self-reliant peasantry of the North-West the system of village communities might be expected to prevail, and did prevail from very ancient times; but in a country like Bengal where climatic and other influences have rendered the people so imbecile and incapable of resistance, every official vested with authority is likely to turn oppressive and tyrannical without evoking any active opposition from the people. The zemindari system, a system (unlike the village communities) which fosters oppression, is then a result of the national character, and has not been instituted by this or that ruler.

These arguments and many more that might be adduced justify us in supposing that a system similar to the zemindari system, (by what name it was called it does not much matter) prevailed in Bengal under the Hindu rulers. We are further justified in assuming that the supreme authority in the realm scarcely or never interfered with the acts and doings of the subordinate officers,—that the people virtually remained in complete servitude under these officers. When such absolute powers are lodged in the hands of such subordinate officers, all the motives which ordinarily lead men to strive to better their condition are taken away from the peasantry, for unless there is at least a tolerable certainty of our enjoying tomorrow what we save to-day all abstinence is folly and foresight useless. The peasantry of Bengal, therefore, it may be asserted as a fact, have never deprived themselves of a single comfort in order to *save*, and have always lived from hand to mouth. And yet among patriarchal nations, there is always found a feeling of reciprocal kindness which tempers the otherwise harsh relationship between masters and servants;—and the peasantry of Bengal, though perhaps living in complete and helpless dependence on their zemindars, were probably better off than one would imagine in the present day.

From these conjectures we come to facts. The Pathans, under Bukhtear Khiliji conquered Bengal in 1203 and remained the rulers of the country till 1576 A. D., in which year the last Pathan King died, and the country was conquered by the Moghuls. The system of government introduced by the Pathans may in some respects be compared with the feudal institutions of Europe.* The king of the country kept one or two chosen districts for himself and distributed the rest among his brother chiefs, who were bound to assist him with arms and money in times of war. These powerful chiefs sometimes paid homage to the king of the country, but whenever they found an opportunity, asserted their independence in their respective districts. Instances too are by no means uncommon of these chiefs electing a king on the demise of

* Stewart's *History of Bengal.*

the preceding ruler. The Hindus of the country, though they were deficient in military skill, were noted for their shrewdness and business-like talents, and the rulers made a good use of such talents. They were employed as zemindars to levy rent from the people; they were employed in responsible posts; they were courted for pecuniary aid in times of war. Thus the Hindu interests in the country were by no means small or unimportant. Indeed in 1385 A. D., we find a Hindu ascending the throne of Bengal, and his dynasty reigned for forty years without any active opposition from the Pathan Chiefs and Jaigirdars.

The relation between zemindars and ryots at this time was that of absolute power on the one side and abject servitude on the other. In one word, the ryots lived in complete servitude under the zemindars. If the zemindars were kind and beneficent, the ryots fared well; if they chose to be oppressive, against their oppression there was no remedy. The zemindars decided all disputes among the ryots,—they punished thieves and evil men and kept peace in the country,—they were virtually the rulers of the people. It is possible the ryots under such circumstances were tolerably well off, but that they should ever improve their circumstances or learn to save was absolutely impossible; and the poor ryot revenged himself by never saving a penny. Remaining in complete ignorance, tilling the land with borrowed capital, powerless to resist and patient under calamities, he lived in his humble cottage and tilled his fertile lands much in the way in which he lives and tills even now. The very seed he sows is borrowed, and oftentimes he lives on borrowed capital for eleven months in the year paying his debts on the twelfth month, and then beginning to borrow again. Surely a more effective way to thwart the cupidity of oppressors has never been invented by a powerless people. Would they intrude into his houses? A mud cabin to shelter him which, if broken down, might be rebuilt in the course of a few days, a handful of corn for his daily food, a couple of cows and a plough, a few earthen utensils and a tattered mat, —these were almost all he possessed and all he required. And with this "he led a life of ease, he loitered and danced and sang. There is no Magistracy in Asia to prevent that."*

Since the conquest of Bengal by the Moghuls, repeated attempts were made by the rulers to put a limit to the power of the zemindars, and to place the revenue of the country on a permanent basis. Of these repeated attempts the most renowned were those of Todar Mall and Murshed Kooly Khan. Todar Mall, immediately after his final conquest of Bengal in 1580 A. D., made *khas* settlement with the ryots for the payment of rent into the imperial treasury. In making this settlement he was no doubt actuated by the impression that the creation of any intermediate agency would entail a loss of revenue,

* *Observations on India, by a Resident there 20 years.*

and might therefore be dispensed with. How long the system he inaugurated continued we do not know for certain, but it is not difficult to understand that in a country like Bengal, several hundreds of miles from the capital of Mahommedan emperors, and where the ryots were so unresisting, the zemindars would soon succeed in coming to their pristine position and power. Later on, therefore, we find the zemindars of the country increasing in power and importance in proportion to the decline of the ruling power. It would seem that in earlier times there were canongoes all over the provinces,—from the pettiest village to the capital of the subadar who formed an efficient check on the conduct of the zemindars and subadars of Bengal. The village canongoes kept accounts relating to harvests and rents, and ascertained what amount every ryot had to pay to his taluqdar or zemindar, and the zemindars of the days of Todar Mall would probably have found it difficult to act in disregard of the accounts of these then important officials. In the same way the Head Canongoe at Murshedabad was the Finance Minister of the provinces, and no accounts could be sent by the Subadar to the Emperor of Hindustan without bearing the seal of this official. In course of time, however, the more centralized power of the zemindars effected a decadence of every independent institution, and the canongoes who at one time were a check on the zemindars came to share the common fate and became paid servants of the zemindars.

The next important attempt made to curb the power of the zemindars was by the tyrannical Murshed Kooly Khan, on and before 1722 A. D. A large portion of the zemindars seem to have held lands not directly under the Subadar of Bengal, but under the Jaigirdars or military chiefs to whom districts or portions of districts were assigned by the Subadar. The revenue, homage and military service of the zemindars were due to these Jaigirdars, in the same way as the homage and service of these Jaigirdars were due to the Subadar. Murshed Kooly as Dewan of Azeem Ooshwan wanted to increase the revenue of the country, but feared a staunch opposition from the powerful Jaigirdars. He therefore transferred the Jaigirdars to Orissa, and thus brought the Hindu zemindars directly under the Subadar. It is easy to imagine that this measure enabled him to increase the revenue of the country at his pleasure. This was in 1701 A. D.

When Murshed Kooly Khan became the Subadar of Bengal, he increased the revenue of the country yet further. He imprisoned all the principal zemindars of the country, without any fault of theirs, and was thus enabled to make a searching enquiry into the actual amount paid by the farmers and cultivators, and declared the *whole* as due to the State. " He ordered the whole of the lands to be remeasured and having ascertained the quantity of fallow and waste ground belonging to every village, he caused a considerable portion of it to be brought into cultivation; for which purpose the Collectors were authorized to make advances to the lower order of husbandmen to purchase stock and reimburse themselves by a certain portion of the produce."* He made collections through his Amils, disallowing the zemindars from having any hand in the collection rent from the cultivators; assigning to them only small allowances either in land or money for their subsistence. This was called the *nánkar* (*nán* in Persian means bread,) and to this was added the *Bankar* (*Ban*—forest) and *julkar* (*jul*—water.) He further inflicted barbarous cruelties and nameless insults on the zemindars, and thus raised the revenue to a crore and a half.†

"The collections of the preceding year were always completed by the end of Chyt; and in the beginning of Bysakh (the first month of the new year) the Nabab generally despatched to Delhi the royal revenue, amounting to one crore and thirty lacs to one crore and fifty lacs of rupees, the greater part in specie. The boxes of treasure were laden upon two hundred or more carts drawn by bullocks, and escorted by a guard of 300 cavalry and 500 infantry, accompanied by one of the sub-treasurers. Along with the revenue he sent, as pre-

* Stewart's History of Bengal.

† The Revenue of Bengal and Orissa has steadily increased.

At the time of Todar Mall	(1582)	it was Rs.	1,06,93,152
" Sultan Suja	(1650)	" "	1,31,15,907
" Murshed Kooly	(1722)	" "	1,52,45,561
" Lord Minto	(1812)	" "	2,02,00,000

This does not include the Revenue of Behar.

sents to the Emperor and ministers, a number of Elephants, hill horses, antelopes, hawks, shields made of rhinoceros hides, sword blades, Sylhet mats, filigree work of gold and silver, wrought ivory, Dacca muslins, and Cossimbazar silks, also a number of European articles procured at the royal port of Hugly.

"The Nabab, attended by his principal officers, accompanied the convoy some miles from Murshedabad, and in order to take off any further responsibility from himself, independent of his own despatches to the vizir, he had the event recorded in the Royal Gazettes, by which all the governors on the route were apprized of the circumstance, and were obliged by the regulations to have carts and an escort ready to forward the treasure to the capital;—those of Bengal being relieved at Patna, and those of the latter place at Allahabad; the convoy and its value frequently increasing as it went on, by the collections of each province."*

The attempts however of Todar Mall and Murshed Kooly Khan to curb the power of the zemindars were ineffectual; for a time the zemindars were certainly reduced in power and importance, but they failed not in the course of a few scores of years to rise again to their pristine glory. We have elsewhere stated that the zemindari system is not the creation of this or that particular ruler but the result of the national character.

* Stewart's History of Bengal.

A more signal and satisfactory proof to establish this fact can scarcely be produced than the repeated failures of the ruling authorities to crush the system. We have seen that in 1722, Murshed Kooly Khan had by unheard of acts of tyranny attempted to annihilate the power and prestige of the zemindars;—a generation scarce passed away before we find them once more possessing a degree of power which they seldom exercised before. During the reign of Surajudowla, and the last days of his predecessor Ali Verdi Khan, the zemindars were rather princes and feudatory chiefs than rent collectors; and one zemindar Rani Bhabani ruled over territories from Dinajpore to the confines of Mymensing and Faridpore.

So long as the zemindars were not defaulters in matters of revenue, they were generally speaking left supreme within their respective territories armed with complete civil and military powers over the people whom they governed. We have a very interesting account* of the manner in which zemindars paid rent into the Subadar's Treasury. "The country was distributed amongst zemindars and Taluqdars who paid a stipulated revenue by twelve instalments to the sovereign power or its delegates. They assembled at the capital in the beginning of every Bengali year (commencing in April) in order to complete their final payments, and make up their annual

* Written by Boughton Rouse in 1791.

accounts; to settle the discount to be charged upon their several remittances in various coins for the purpose of reducing them to one standard or adjust their concerns with the bankers; to petition for remissions on account of storms, drought, inundation, disturbances and the like; and to make their representations of the state and occurrences of their districts; after all which they entered upon the collections of the new year, of which however they were not permitted to begin receiving the rents from the farmers till they had completely closed the accounts of the preceding year, so that they might not encroach upon the new rents to make up the deficiency of the past."

It was a great thing in those days to have sufficient influence in the Subadar's Court; and for this purpose every well-to-do zemindar had a representative in the Court to soothe the vanity of the Subadar or his ministers with flattery, or satisfy their cupidity with occasional presents. Instances were not uncommon of estates being taken away by the Subadar from one zemindar, and transferred to a more favored individual. Still however the hereditory character of zemindars was generally recognized,* and even when they were deprived of their estates for default of payment or for not having sufficient influence in Court, such estates were in most cases granted to some other member of the same family. This kind

* See the articles on Territorial Aristocracy in Bengal by the late Baboo Kissory Chand Mitter.

and considerate conduct on the part of the ruling power excited an interest in the zemindars in the well being of their *hereditary* estates and subjects, and inspired some confidence in the people in their *hereditary* masters. And when we add to this the fact that among all patriarchal nations, among whom the ideas of law and right are imperfectly understood, the *custom of the land* is pleaded, and pleaded not in vain, against excessive exactions, and is often considered inviolate even by oppressive masters,—we are inclined to the belief that acts of oppression or harassing exactions were not of such frequent occurrence as they might have been. While therefore it were idle to deny that power unchecked is invariably power abused, and abused grossly in such a country as Bengal, it is still to be hoped, that matters were not quite so bad as they might otherwise have been.

It is the curse of oriental governments that the beneficence or generosity of a good ruler hardly if ever affects the interests of the people, whose happiness almost entirely depends on the will of their immediate superiors. It is at the same time the blessing of such governments that the oppressiveness of tyrants often leaves the people untouched, and like the waves of an angry sea contents itself with striking against the rocks and pillars of the state. While the cruel Surajudowla was robbing his bankers and rich zemindars, the cultivators of an extensive tract of country from Dinajpur to the confines of Mymensing and Faridpur were basking under the humane reign of the munificent Rani Bhabáni. The oppressiveness of Surajudowla did not leave her unscathed,—it is said he purposed to violate the chastity of her widowed daughter Tárá, then in the bloom of her youthful beauty, but the viceregal wrath went no further. Rani Bhabáni's subjects were blessed with daily increasing alms-houses and *Atithi-Salas* and lakhraj lands. History in oriental countries,—history to a certain extent in all countries—has been written on a wrong principle. We are repeatedly called upon to admire the generosity of princes who shower blessings and favors on the favorites and Omrahs of the Court, to wonder at their conquests and victories, to feel astonished at the temples and towers which at their command beautify their metropolis. We are repeatedly called upon to execrate the Emperors who have lost kingdoms by their folly or disgusted the nobility with their cruelty or avarice;—and this is the sum total of oriental history. The toiling masses of humanity peopling villages and towns, growing year after year the rice and the wheat by which the vast and towering fabric of a mighty empire is supported, manufacturing year after year those articles of use or luxury by which the commerce and the fame of the country are maintained,—they find no place even in the back ground of a false colored picture called History. If, instead of these nameless and senseless annals of crime and folly, we had a correct portraiture of the condition of the people, we should find that even under the best Emperors and Subadars the people suffered under the chronic oppression of officers and zemindars, and that often under the worst rulers, their mad cruelties did not reach the people.

Except, then, on very rare occasions. the zemindars of the country were the absolute rulers of the people in all revenue matters. They were not less so in criminal and judicial matters, at least during the last days of Mahommedan rule in Bengal. There were a few courts in the capital of the country, and probably also at some large towns, but in the interior of the country the zemindars decided all disputes among the ryots, and exercised criminal powers to the extent of hanging offenders. It was their duty not only to collect rent from the people but to keep the peace of the country, to chastise thieves and robbers, and to quell insurgents and traitors. Our readers will excuse us if, while on this subject, we make the following somewhat long extract from a very interesting letter dated 15th August 1772, addressed by the Committee of Circuit to the Council at Fort William.*

"The general principle of all despotic governments, that every degree of power shall be simple and undivided, seems necessarily to have introduced itself into the Courts of Justice; and this will appear from a review

---

* The letter is quoted in the Administration Report of Bengal, Registration Department, 1872-73.

of the different officers of justice instituted in these provinces. * * *

"*1st.*—The Nazim as supreme Magistrate presides personally in the trials of capital offenders and holds a court every Sunday called the Raz Adawlat.

"*2nd.*—The Dewan is the supposed Magistrate for the decision of such causes as relate to real estates or property in land, but seldom exercises this authority in person.

"*3rd.*—The Darogah Adawlat at Aalea is properly the Deputy of the Nazim; he is the judge of all matters of property, excepting claims of land and inheritance. He also takes cognizance of quarrels, frays and abusive names.

"*4th.*—The Darogah Adawlat Dewani or Deputy of the Dewan is the judge of property in land.

"*5th.*—The Fouzdar is the officer of the Police, the Judge of all crimes not capital; the proofs of these last are taken before him and reported to the Nazim for his judgment and sentence upon them.

"*6th.*—The Kazi is the judge of all claims of inheritance or succession, he also performs the ceremonies of weddings, circumcision and funerals.

"*7th.*—The Mohtesib has cognizance of drunkenness, and of the vending of spirituous liquors, and intoxicating drugs, and the examination of false weights and measures.

"8*th*.—The Muftee is the expounder of the law. The Kazi is assisted by the Muftee and Mohtesib in his court. After hearing the parties and evidences the Muftee writes the Fettwa or the law applicable to the case in question, and the Kazi pronounces judgment accordingly. If either the Kazi or Mohtesib disapprove of the fettwa the cause is referred to the Nazim, who summons the ejlass or general assembly, consisting of the Kazi, Muftee, Mohtesib, the Darogahs of the Adawlut, the Moulvies and all the learned in the law to meet and decide upon it. Their decision is final.

"9*th*.—The Canongoes are the Registrars of the lands. They have no authority, but causes of lands are often referred to them for decision by the Nazim or Dewan or Darogah of the Dewani.

"10*th*.—The Cotwall is the peace officer of the night, dependent on the Fouzdari.*

* * * * * * *

"Another great and capital defect in these courts is the want of a substitute or subordinate jurisdiction for the distribution of justice in such parts of the province as lie out of their reach, which in effect confines their operations to a circle extending but a small distance beyond the bounds of the city of Murshedabad. This indeed is not universally the case; but perhaps it will not be difficult to prove the exceptions to be an accumu-

* We need scarcely remind our readers that these courts were held only in the capital of Bengal.

lation of the grievance, since it is true that the Courts of Adawlat are open to the complaints of all men, yet it is only the rich or the vagabond part of the people who can afford to travel so far for justice; and if the industrious laborer is called from the farthest part of the province to answer their complaints and wait the tedious process of the courts to which they are thus made amenable, the consequences in many cases will be more ruinous and oppressive than an arbitrary decision could be, if passed against them without any law or process whatever.

"This defect is not, however, left absolutely without a remedy; the zemindars, farmers, shekdars and other officers of the revenue assuming that power for which no provision is made by the laws of the land, but which in whatever manner it is exercised is preferable to total anarchy. It will however be obvious that the judicial authority, lodged in the hands of men who gain their livelihood on the profits on the collections of the revenue, must unavoidably be converted to sources of private emolument; and in effect the greatest oppressions to the inhabitants owe their origin to this necessary evil. The Kazi has also his substitutes in the districts, but their legal powers are too limited to be of general use, and the powers which they assume being warranted by no lawful commission, but depending on their own pleasure or the ability of the people to contest them, is also an oppression."

From the foregoing sketch our readers will probably have derived an idea of the condition of the peasantry of Bengal under the Mahommedan rule. The ryots lived in complete servitude under the zemindars, having no rights except the plea of ancient custom, and no protection from unjust exactions or acts of oppression except such as was to be found in the clemency of the zemindars or their sense of self-interest. The zemindars on the other hand were in the eye of the law as well as of the sovereign, mere rent collectors, charged with keeping peace in the country,—but virtually they were (except on certain occasions) feudatory chiefs, armed with complete civil and criminal powers within the limits of their extensive territories, and bound only to pay a certain stated revenue to the Subadar of the country.

CHAPTER III.

The Bengal Ryot under early English Rule.

> War disguised as commerce came,
> Britain carrying sword and flame,
> Won an empire, lost her name.
>
> Montgomery.

It was in 1757 that a few Mahommedans and Hindus, oppressed beyond endurance by a capricious and tyrannical despot, called to their aid a band of foreign traders to dethrone the Subadar. The idea was not repugnant to the feelings of these ambitious traders, and they lent a willing ear to the proposal. More than a century has rolled away, and those Hindus and Mahommedans have long ceased to live. Were it possible for them to awake from their long sleep, they would indeed have reason to wonder and to pride on the wisdom of their choice. Instead of a country desolated by long misrule, harassed by frequent invasions, plundered by its own governors, they would view, with delight, peace spreading from one end of the land to the other, commerce thriving, agriculture spreading, the resources of the country fast developing to a wonderful extent. They would see their beautiful country dotted with fair and spacious towns, and their countrymen fast possessing themselves of sciences and a literature freer and nobler than even what their renowned ancestors could lay claim to. Last, though not the least, instead of a general system of oppression by almost every recipient of power resulting in a general insecurity of life and property, they would wonder to see an amount of security and freedom unheard of in the annals of India,—a freedom which allows us not only to act as we please but even to think and say what we please, though it be against our rulers themselves. A contemplation of the past is always instructive; and though it is but meet and proper that, imbibing the liberal ideas of our rulers, we should criticise their acts judged by *their* ideas of justice, it is also meet that we should not altogether lose sight of what we were a hundred years ago,—that we should not be altogether unmindful of the blessings secured to us by the British Rule,—that we should not be altogether wanting in gratitude to those who have so blessed us.

But it is not about the general improvement that we here intend to speak. Our subject is the condition of the peasantry and the peasantry alone. In the next chapter we shall see that in some respects the cultivating classes have shared in the general improvement, that the correct and liberal principles of English administration in Bengal have caused an awakening among the peasantry from a long sleep of servitude. But this result was not obtained in a day. We shall therefore, in the present chapter, briefly dwell on the early acts and frequent mistakes of the British in Bengal, and then proceed to later events.*

The Revenue Administration of Bengal was made over to the English by the treaty of 1765, A. D. From 1765 A. D. up to 1772 A. D. the Company did their work in disguise, employing native collectors to collect rent as heretofore. A body of professedly trading adventurers, as they were, they did not yet venture to step forward as the administrators of the country. This system, however, was productive of gross evils, to remedy

* Dr. Hunter, in one of the most brilliant chapters of his Annals of Rural Bengal, traces the changes in administration introduced in Bengal in the last century.

which the Company had recourse to employing European servants. This policy, as might have been expected, utterly failed to bring about the wished-for result, specially as the supervisors were few in number, and quite unacqainted with the customs and manners of the people. This state of things contimued till the year 1772 saw the commencement of the vigorous administration of Warren Hastings. That earnest man realized the true position of the Company not as a band of traders in the East, but as the rulers of a vast empire which had fallen into their hands from the nerveless grasp of the Moghuls. He tore the mask asunder, and from 1772 the Company boldly stood forth as the revenue collectors of the country.

For a time, however, matters were changed from bad to worse, and the first attempts of the English at revenue administration resulted in ignominious failure. The Mahommedans, with their thorough knowledge of the country and its people, shaped their demands in accordance with the circumstances. We have seen before that they made remissions on account of every circumstance which made the zemindar really unable to pay rent, and yet such remissions could not lead to fraud as the officers of state were thoroughly acquainted with the real condition of every zemindar. The English not only lacked this knowledge, but they came from Europe impressed with the idea of an almost religious strictness in the discharge of dues between subjects and sovereigus—and they would therefore hear of no excuse for remission. Some estates, too, happened to be assessed at an exorbitant rate which could not be paid, and severities and cruelties followed. Defaulting zemindars were treated with barbarous vigour, and sent down to Calcutta one by one under escort, and were often confined under a guard of sepoys. Puzzled and perplexed at being required to pay rent with a punctuality and strictness never known before, the zemindars had to dispose of estate after estate; some were ruined, all lost their prestige. That hereditary attachment which, one may hope, prevailed in former times between zemindars and ryots was destroyed for ever. Still bitterer consequences followed. The estates were broken up and sold at auction to swarms of *lotdars* and absentees, who had no kind of interest in the welfare of the estates, no hereditary affection for the people, no regard for any custom which might have prevailed under former zemindars, and whose only object therefore was to screw up the demands on the people to pay the demands of the Government, and to heap new claims and cruelties on the devoted head of an unfortunate peasantry.

The Civil Administration of Bengal was never formally made over to the English, nor specially reserved by the Nabob in 1765. We have seen before that under the Mahommedans there were only a few civil courts in the capital of the province, the mass of civil cases in the moffusil being decided by zemindars and others who had sufficient power and prestige in the country. This state of things continued from 1765 to 1772 in which year the English Government under the vigorous administration of Warren Hastings became alive to their duties. The measures taken were however exceedingly inadequate, there were only a very few civil courts in the country, and the office of Judge formed a part and a very small and unimportant part of the Collector's duty;—a significant fact, shewing that the East India Company, true to their vocation as traders, cared far more for their own profits than for the welfare of the people brought under their rule. To give the modern reader an idea as to how civil justice was administered in those times, it is enough to mention the single fact that ryots who had the hardihood to seek justice in those days had sometimes to wait over a score of years before they could obtain a verdict. While on the one hand the English, by destroying the power and prestige of the zemindars, destroyed the only instrument for the administration of civil justice in Bengal, they were themselves too slow to come forward and supply the desideratum thus created. A state of anarchy followed, and the strong oppressed the weak with all the licentious audacity that marks such times of misrule.

The Criminal Administration of Bengal was specially reserved by the Nabob by the treaty of 1765, and for this duty he was paid a sum of £360,000 over and above the personal allowance of £ 180,000 assigned to him by the same treaty. The Nabob, however, left the duty wholly unperformed, and consequently there was no regular criminal administration of the country till the English took it up in 1790, A. D.

It will be seen that the government of the Mahommedans had two main functions to discharge, *viz.*, the protection of the country from all external enemies and insurgents, and the collection of revenue. The Subadar of Bengal was expected by the Emperor of Hindustan to protect the country against all enemies, and to send an annual instalment of rent to Delhi. In the same way every zemindar was expected to defend his territories from traitors and insurgents, and to send on the fixed quota of revenue. The Emperor of Delhi did not concern himself as to how justice was administered in a distant Subadaree, and the Subadar cared as little as to how justice was administered in a distant zemindaree. A new principle was introduced with the advent of the English; a third duty—that of the administration of justice—was taken up by Government, and we believe it was a correct principle. Posterity cannot but contemplate with pleasure this salutary change. It has invested the imperial Government with a duty which ought never to be made a handmaid to the powers of any particular class of people,—it has in the present day almost entirely closed the gates of corruption among judicial officers,—it has rendered justice between zemindars and ryots possible for the first time in the history of Bengal—it has inspired the peasantry with confidence and freed them from that unwholesome servitude in thought and action under the zemindars, which the constitution of the Mahommedan Government necessitated and perpetuated.

But, though at this distance of time the depriving of the zemindars of their prestige and magisterial powers appears a beneficial act, the immediate consequences were baneful in the extreme. Indeed, the misery of the *people* (and not of the influential few) about the end of the 18th century, so graphically described by Macaulay, began not with the reign of the inhuman Surajudowla as has been represented by historians, but with the transfer of these provinces to the English. And the reason lies in a nutshell. A handful of alien conquerors found that the institutions, social and political, in Bengal were not exactly such as they would choose or even could tolerate, and they rashly demolished them before they could put up any thing in their stead. Justice was administered in the country tolerably or indifferently before the advent of the English, the new comers deprived the zemindars of that office before they knew how to administer it themselves. The first attempts proved abortive in the extreme. Young magistrates,—we hope not all of the stamp of Joe Sedley, unacquainted or but imperfectly acquainted with the language of the country—were surrounded by Amlahs and the all-powerful Serishtadar who literally sold justice to the highest bidders.

Gangs of dacoits pillaged the country without there being a chance of detection, for the Serishtadar was deeply bribed, and often sheltered sardar dacoits, being himself the receiver of stolen property. The traditions of Bengal are to the present day replete with the fearful remembrances of the last century, and the names of some of the renowned dacoits have passed into bye-words. As regards the early efforts of the police, their extortion and fearful oppression are but too well-known; and it is not perhaps an exaggeration to say that in those days a dacoity was less feared on its own account than on account of the police investigation that was to follow. Old men in the present day remember the time when shops were closed, treasures were buried, cattle driven into jungles; and villages deserted, when a police investigation was anticipated.

Manufactures declined, and manufacturers sank into poverty. Trade, which was never prosperous in Bengal under a system of harassing inland duties under the Mahommedans, found a new obstacle in the general insecurity of the times, and a still more powerful one in the competition of the Company's servants who ignoring all claims of justice, and laying aside the strict orders of their masters as so much waste paper, were amassing large fortunes in the twinkling of an eye and returning millionaries to their wondering friends in England. Under these accumulated calamities, the ties that bind society were almost ready to burst, and a convulsive disorganization was almost ready to ensue. It would have ensued in the shape of a general revolution among any other people than the Bengalis, who are so tenacious to order, so persistent in their inactivity, so strong in passive resistance, that nothing has ever produced or shall produce a social explosion among them. Such was the inauspicious beginning of English rule in Bengal.*

In 1772 the English formally stood forth as the Dewan of Bengal, and in the same year a Committee of Circuit was appointed consisting of a President (Mr. Hastings) and four other members of Government to go about through the province of Bengal to make a new settlement. *Amalnámás* were given by the Committee to protect the ryots from arbitrary exactions. The contents of the *Amalnámás* shew that zemindari oppression was the crying grievance of the day. Section II of the *Amalnámás* runs thus :—"You are to let the rates of

---

* Dr. Hunter gives us a pleasing picture of the condition of the ryots in the "Company's villages," *i.e.*, those villages which the Company had taken under their special patronage for trading purposes. The country was yet too poor to produce on its own capital goods fit for the European market, and so the Company's servants had to advance capital to the weavers and workmen, much in the same way in which European planters and silk manufacturers do in our days. These villages were jealously guarded, and while the open country was pillaged at pleasure by gangs of banditti, the fiercest of them would turn away with a shrug from the tempting and prosperous weaving villages of the Company. It must be remembered however that the number of Company's villages bore an insignificant and scarcely perceptible proportion to the entire number of villages in Bengal. Of the desolate condition of the country in general Macaulay gives a more correct description.

the former Malguzari and the Pottah for the present year's cultivation be the standard of your collections from the ryots; should it be known that you exact more, you will not only have to repay the ryots the sums which you have so exacted, but also make a proportional forfeiture to Government, and if it be represented that you are a second time guilty of any oppression on the ryots, your farms will be made *khas* and you shall pay a fine to Government."

We have seen that in earlier days the Canangoes were an efficient check on the zemindar's conduct and exactions, and Mr. Hastings made an attempt to restore them to their former efficiency and to re-establish the ancient revenue system of the country, "which by its useful checks from the accountant assessors of the village through its several gradations upwards to the Accountant General of the exchequer was no less calculated to protect the great body of the people from oppression than to secure the full and legal rights of the Sovereign." Such were the able measures proposed by Mr. Hastings to improve the condition of the Bengal peasantry. Unfortunately he was too soon succeeded by another Governor-General more generous and benevolent, but utterly devoid of that shrewdness and business-like talent that marked Warren Hastings.

The generous soul of Lord Cornwallis was distressed at the accounts he daily received of the misery of the peasantry of Bengal about the end of the 18th century which we have described before. Justice was badly administered or not administered at all, those who were the ancient administrators of justice, the old zemindars, were either swept away from their possessions or had lost prestige. New men who had stepped into their places by purchase were heaping new cruelties on the people in order to pay the exorbitant rates at which the estates had been assessed. Crime went unpunished, and dacoity and gang robbery impoverished an already poor country and snapped the strings of industry and trade. Lord Cornwallis at once resolved on redress.

This was a critical moment. It was a moment that comes but once in the history of a nation, a moment whose good use might have compensated for the misrule of generations. The Bengal ryot, passionately fond of his home and his land, had not ceased to cultivate it in spite of all misrule and oppression, and the moment had come when his unfailing interest in his land might have been rewarded by vesting him with its proprietorship, or at least by granting him long lease on a fixed rent. He had suffered most cruelly in those oppressive times, and the moment had come when the long tissue of his grievances might have been redressed by making him the little zemindar of his land. He had for centuries groaned under the oppression of the zemindar,—and the moment had come when the zemindars might have been turned adrift and an end put to the oppression of centuries. But this was not to be. The moment was lost, and once lost it has been lost for ever. The prodigious blunder of Lord Cornwallis ought to be a living warning against all hasty legislation, specially by alien legislators.

It is needless to bring forward arguments to prove that under the Mahommedan regime the right of property belonged exclusively to the State. We have seen before that the zemindars of those days, though powerful within their territories, were, in point of law, mere rent-collectors, were frequently changed by the Subadars of Bengal; and in some instances were actually imprisoned, the collection of rent being taken off from their hands and given to other officers of State. The English on coming to India, therefore, came to be invested with that right of property in land; and "the generous resolution was adopted of sacrificing to the improvement of country the proprietory rights of the Sovereign. The motives to improvement which property gives, and of which the power was so justly appreciated, might have been bestowed upon those, upon whom they would have operated with a force incomparably greater than that with which they could operate upon any other class of men; they might have been bestowed upon those from whom alone in every country the principal improvements in agriculture must be derived—the immediate cultivators of the soil. And a measure worthy to be ranked among the noblest that ever were taken for the improvement of any country might have helped to compensate the people of India for the miseries of that misgovernment they had so long endured"* But Lord Cornwallis was an aristocrat, and aristocratic prejudices prevailed. In vain did Mr. Shore urge upon him the fact that by such a settlement the ryots were left at the mercy of their hereditary oppressors,—in vain did he argue that the proposed settlement precisely left unredressed the grievance whose redress it contemplated. His lordship was too deeply impressed with the necessity and importance of the PERMANENT SETTLEMENT OF BENGAL to brook resistance or delay. In 1793 A. D., the regulation was passed. The right of property was given not to the cultivators but to their hereditary oppressors,—with the expectation that, armed with this new right, they would refrain from oppression!

And how fared the ryots? By a gross negligence (or was it malice aforethought?) Lord Cornwallis refrained from putting in a single section to check zemindari exactions or to define the rights of the cultivators. The earlier revenue system of Bengal contained distinct provisions to save ryots from oppression, and Mr. Hastings had attempted to revive the ancient system by his measure about Canangoe Dufters. But Lord Cornwallis would have none of it. He virtually ignored all rights of the cultivators (Istemraree and Mucarraree ryots excepted) and as if to give the zemindars the freest scope for extortion actually disestablished the

* Mill's *History of British India*, Bk. vi. Chap. 5.

Canongoe Dufter system of his predecessor. Seldom in the annals of any country has hasty legislation been productive of effects so calamitous as the ill-conceived Permanent Settlement. On the head of Lord Cornwallis will rest the blame, that the extortion of the zemindars and their underlings has not to the present day ceased—that the ill feeling between the ryot and his master has advanced with the advance of years. On his lordship's head will rest the guilt, that the most fertile source of revenue in a fertile country has been closed up for ever,—that the extension of cultivation has increased, not the wealth of the cultivators, but the number of a class of impoverished idlers, tho zemindars with a two anna or one anna share of the ancestral estate. On his lordship's head rests the blame, that we do not yet see the faintest glimmerings of rural civilization, that the ryot of the present day is as thoughtless and improvident a creature as he was centuries ago, despite the notions of enlightenment imported from the west, despite the energetic efforts of English administration to remedy the defect.

And yet the Act was, we believe, passed with the best of intentions. Says section VII of the Act—"To conduct themselves with good faith and moderation towards their dependant taluqdars and ryots are duties at all times indispensably required from the proprietors of land, and a strict observance of these rules is now more than ever incumbent on them in return for the benefits which they will themselves derive from the orders now passed. *The Governor-General in Council therefore expects that the proprietors of lands will not only act in this manner themselves towards their dependant taluqdars and ryots,* BUT ALSO ENJOIN THE STRICTEST ADHERENCE TO THE SAME PRINCIPLES ON THE PERSONS WHOM THEY MAY APPOINT TO COLLECT THE RENT FROM THEM." The Italics and Capitals are our own: but have the expectations of the Governor-General been realized? Painful experience, broad daylight facts, prove the contrary.

It was not long before the measure began to produce its bitter but legitimate fruits, and received universal condemnation from the British public. It would fill a volume to quote at length the opinions of eminent statesmen matured by long residence and experience in this country; but as specimens we shall extract a very few.

The Court of Directors, writing in 1819, complained "that, if the policy of Mr. Hastings had not been departed from, or if a stop had not been put to the further prosecution of Mr. Grant's valuable labors, we should not now have to lament that the object of the Permanent Settlement, in so far as regards the security and happiness of the most numerous and industrious class of the community, have hitherto been so imperfectly attained, that instead of maintaining their rights we have not ascertained what they are."* In the same

* Reveuue letter to Bengal &c., 15th January 1819. Para 38.

Despatch they add "that consequences, the most injurious to the rights and interests of individuals, have arisen from describing those with whom the Permanent Settlement was concluded as the *actual proprietors of lands*."* Lord Moira, alluding to zemindari oppressions, ascribed them to the very same cause, and asserts that "the cause of this is to be traced to the incorrectness of principle assumed at the time of the Perpetual Settlement when those with whom Government entered into engagements were declared the sole proprietors of the soil."† "Never," says Lord Hastings, "was there a measure conceived with a purer spirit of generous humanity and disinterested justice than the plan for the Permanent Settlement in the lower provinces. It was worthy the soul of a Cornwallis—yet this truly benevolent purpose, fashioned with great care and deliberation, has to our painful knowledge subjected almost the whole of the lower provinces to the most grievous oppression; an oppression, too, so guaranteed by our pledge that, we are unable to relieve the sufferers."‡ "The errors" says Sir E. Colebrooke, "of the Settlement are two-fold; first, in the sacrifice of what might be denominated the yeomanry by merging all tillage rights, whether of property or of occupancy, in the all-devouring recognition of the zemindar's premanent property in the soil; and

* Ibid. Para 54.
† Minute dated 21st September 1815. Para 141.
‡ Minute dated 31st December 1819.

then leaving the zemindar to make his settlement with the peasantry as he might choose to require." But we must be tiring our readers with extracts.

Not only has British legislation ignored in the Permanent Settlement all rights of the cultivating classes, but it has also been sadly negligent in redeeming the only pledge it gave them as a feeble compensation for the injustice done. The Permanent Settlement declares that "it being the duty of the ruling power to protect all classes of people and more particularly those who from their situation are most helpless," it would be competent to the Governor General in Council to "enact such regulations as he may think necessary for the protection and welfare of the defendant taluqdars, ryots and other cultivators of the soil."* Has any such regulation been enacted? Has the pledge been redeemed?

Four scores of years have rolled away since the Permanent Settlement,—what fruits have these eighty years of active legislation borne for the poor ryot? Echo answers what? Within this period a world of salutary legislation has reformed every department and every institution,—but whom does this concern?—Not the millions of the peasantry of Bengal whose history of these eighty years presents us with a cheerless blank. Commerce has thriven, but commerce to them is practically forbidden; and if agriculture has been extended, the zemindars and not the ryots reap the blessings. That servitude under

* Sec. viii of Act I. of 1793.

which the ryots have groaned for centuries has now been rudely shaken, as we shall shew in the next chapter; but it has been shaken not through salutary legislation,—it has been shaken despite adverse legislation. In all other respects the ryot still lives as his forefathers lived, in ignorance and poverty, and yet finding time in the vacant routine of his every day life moments to smile and sing with an empty heart and unrepressed hilarity.

Four scores of years have passed away since the Permanent Settlement; we shall briefly trace the steps taken within this period to improve the condition of the ryots.

Lord Cornwallis was succeeded by Lord Wellesley as the Governor-General of India, and as if to mock the misfortunes of the peasantry he passed coercive measures to subject the persons and property of the peasantry to the tender mercies of the zemindar! It is impossible even in the present day,—after the lapse of the best half of a century,—to turn to the first fruits of English legislation in Bengal without a feeling of sadness and shame at the unfortunate manner in which the interests of the millions of Bengal were regarded and served by those to whom alone they could look up for protection. History describes with fulsome praise the administration of Lord Wellesley, and no doubt so long as mankind will continue to gape with silly admiration at martial triumphs and unprincipled annexations, Lord Wellesley will be lauded and worshipped. But the impartial and candid student of history will not fail to observe that Lord Wellesley's reign is but one long tissue of the most unjust and oppressive warfare, extortion, and annexation. He was wrong in the war with Mysore, wrong in the war with the Mahrattas, grossly wrong in his interference with Oude. If an aristocrat, who regarded unprincipled vigour as the one means of good administration, betrayed a total want of sympathy for the plebeians of plebeians,—the ryots of the country,—is it a matter of wonder?

But there was a still lower depth to which English legislation could descend. The Board of Revenue received from Collectors and transmitted to Government harrowing accounts of zemindari oppression, and yet no one knew how there could be any redress. A fatal fear seems to have seized every one lest the so-called "right of property" of the zemindars were interfered with, and every proposal therefore of saving the ryots, and setting some limit to zemidari oppression fell through. At last almost in utter despair, Mr. Colebrooke proposed that "it "would be better to abrogate most of the laws in favor "of the ryot, and leave him for a certain period to be "specified, under no other protection for his tenure than "the specific terms of the lease which he may hold." This proposal was carried into effect,—but, somehow, no period was specified, and the insane Acts II. and XVIII. of 1812 were the result. They declared in so many words that the ryot had absolutely no rights of occupancy as against the zemindar! It will be difficult in the history of the world to find out another instance of a ruling power so ignominiously failing in the very object of their legislation. Not a year passed without some attempt being made towards the protection of ryots. Despatch after despatch came from the Court of Directors, minute after minute was written by Governors-General, measure after measure proposed, rejected, and proposed again, enquiries set on foot, regulations multiplied beyond number,—and all for the protection and welfare of ryots. And yet the fatality which seemed to hang over the spirit of English legislation ever since Warren Hastings left India, rendered every proposal ineffectual, every attempt abortive.

Nor are the reasons far to seek. Society and politics in Bengal were a contrast to society and politics in England; and rulers were called, as it were, from a distant planet to manage a people surpassing strange in their manners and institutions. In England, there is a spirit of resistance even among the lowest classes which renders gross oppression of the weak by the strong impossible. Half a century of bitter experience failed to convince the alien rulers of Bengal, that such resistance to oppression was utterly wanting among the people, and must therefore *be created by legislation.* English society is surcharged with commercial notions, and whenever a class of people comes in close contact with another, a tacit contract and consequent intercourse arises almost spontaneously between such classes. Half a century of residence in Bengal failed to convince the English legislators, that such spontaneous contract was almost impossible among a patriarchal people with whom every relationship was based on status; and that after having demolished the pre-existing relationship between the zemindar and the ryot, it behove the new rulers to create a fresh relationship by a special act of legislation, and to define the rights and duties,—the status in fact of each of those classes. These reflections which force themselves on us in the present day were impossible in those days. On the contrary, the "right of property" was a bugbear to the early English legislators,—it was a Frankenstein of their creation which threatened and haunted them at every step, proved fatal to all their good intentions, and prevented any action for the relief of the cultivators, notwithstanding that Sec. viii. of Reg. I. of 1793 promised and provided for such action. To such a height was this fatal fear screwed up, that "it may almost be said that at one time, to ask a ryot "his name anywhere but in a court of justice was "considered by some people contrary to the principles "of the Permanent Settlement!" The English have often been accused of want of originality of idea. The charge may be true or it may be false,—but the early history of English legislation in Bengal seems to afford one instance at least of its truth. Half a century of experience in this country did not enable them to rid themselves of certain legal ideas which they had imported from England, or to adapt legislation to the peculiar circumstances of the country.

But it is useless to follow the tedious annals of a vacillating legislation any further; and we shall therefore pass on to the consideration of a strong act by a strong man. It was the man who had the cool courage to preach mercy when all India cried for revenge on the mutineers of 1856—it was Lord Canning who composedly ventured to set at naught the absurd theories built up on the so-called "right of property" of the zemindars, and after a lapse of 66 years to make a really earnest endeavour in his Act X. of 1859 to give effect for the first time to the clause of the Permanent Settlement above referred to.

It is not our purpose to give here a detailed account of this celebrated Act, we shall notice some of its most prominent features. By it the distinctive rights of zemindars and ryots were for the first time, created, and sanctions provided for the proper discharge of such duties. Three classes of ryots were created, viz., (1) Those whose ancestors have held lands since the Permanent Settlement; (2) those who have held lands for 12 years or more; and (3) those who have held lands for any shorter period. Enhancement of rent is impossible so far as the first class of ryots are concerned; and as regards the second class it is allowed only on fair and equitable grounds, *i. e.*, when it is proved that the rent paid by such ryot is less than the prevailing rate, or that the productive powers of his lands have increased otherwise than by his own agency, or that the quantity of his lands is greater than what he ostensibly pays rent for. The third class of ryots were in this respect left entirely at the mercy of the zemindars who can demand any rent from them, and in default of payment send them out of the zemindaree. Similarly, while the first and second class ryots cannot be ousted by the zemindar so long as they pay their proper rent, the third class ryots may be driven away from their homesteads at the will and pleasure of the zemindar.

It will thus be seen that even Act X. of 1859* affords but a feeble protection to the third and most numerous class of ryots; and this is the point on which we would draw the attention of our legislators. We hope we have seen the last of that curious advocacy of the zemindar's rights of property which for over half a century rendered legislation on the subject impossible;—we hope the Government of the present day will not be daunted by such riff-raff arguments from giving the fullest effect to Sec. VIII. of Reg. I. of 1793. The late lamented Mr. Mill advocated the bestowing on the State instead of on the English landlords the increase of revenue which in the natural course of things accrues to every bit of land under cultivation; and his suggession was based on the most spacious

* Now Act VIII. of 1869.

reasons, *viz.*, that a class of idle people should not reap the benefits of an increase which they had not any hand in bringing about. With stronger reason we may advocate the bestowal of the same boon in India, not on the State, but on the cultivators, from whom all improvements in land emanate, and upon whom such a boon will operate as the strongest motive for improving lands.

All that is wanted is the bestowal on the second and third class ryots the rights which have already been secured to the first class,—to prevent them from being ousted of their lands at the will of the zemindar. This will be a befitting completion of the good work commenced by Lord Canning, and the strong ruler who does this will, in Lord Canning's own words, establish "a lasting claim to the gratitude of the cultivators of the soil in Bengal, and to the acknowledgments of all who are interested in their well-being." The Permanent Settlement has been called the Magna Charta of the zemindar's rights. Should an Act secure to the second and third class ryots the rights referred to above,—such an Act will create a more glorious PERMANENT SETTLEMENT (between the zemindars and the ryots) and will form the Magna Charta of a more numerous and useful,—a more industrious and productive,—and withal a worthier class,—to wit the PEASANTRY OF BENGAL.

CHAPTER IV.

THE BENGAL RYOT AT THE PRESENT DAY.

I grant indeed that fields and flocks have charms
For him that grazes and for him that farms;
But when amid such pleasing scenes I trace
The poor laborious natives of the place,
And see the midday sun, with fervid ray,
On their bare heads and dewy temples play;
While some with feebler heads and fainter hearts,
Deplore their fortune, yet sustain their parts,
Then shall I dare these real ills to hide
In tinsel trappings of poetic pride.

CRABBE.

WE stated at the beginning of the preceding chapter that the cultivating classes have in some extent shared in the general improvement of the country. We shall in the present chapter shew in what respects their condition has improved. We shall dwell briefly on their habits and customs, and shall trace the causes through which in spite of mistaken legislation the villagers of the present day are improving in their condition.

To one who has never been out of town, the prospect of the open country must be striking and pleasant. We do not see here the undulating hills and vales, the green pasture lands with sheep and kine grazing on them, and the neat hedgerows and clusters of cheerful looking cottages strewn about here and there that greet the eye of the traveller in England; but in their stead we see on both sides of us extensive paddy fields spreading their sea-like expanse as far as the eye can reach, with waving corn shining under the golden tints of the morning Indian sun,—the scene being hardly checkered by a single tree or bush. Far off the view is bounded by a line of thick vegetation and tangled woods and trees of various kinds, covered with luxuriant foliage. Concealed in the thick shade of this beautiful green canopy of nature, our poor and simple villagers have their clusters of neat though humble dwelling houses. Let us leave the main road, we cross a number of paddy fields, and in about half an hour reach one of the shady villages. It is impossible to describe the calmness and tranquility that reign in this rural scene. The thick canopy of branches and leaves ward off the rays and heat of the sun; solitary foot-paths meander among clusters of neat and low-built cottages; and here and there a stagnant pool, covered with green plants, or full of beautiful lotuses proudly lifting up their heads, attract the attention of the visitor. The only sound audible is the continual rustling of the leaves, and the no less continual voices of birds of various kinds and rich plumage, issuing from bush and tree like a flood of cheerful music. A spot so secluded seems devoted to peace and rural happiness;—alas! it is the home of poverty, suffering, and ignorance.

Our cultivators manifest some skill and shrewdness in the selection of particular kinds of soil adapted to the growth of particular species of crops. Careful distinction is made between high lands for early rice (*aûs*), and low lands for late rice (*aman*); and jute, sugarcane and different kinds of pulse, are also grown on lands adapted for their growth. Still, however, of scientific knowledge in agriculture we have but little, notwithstanding that agriculture is the profession of by far the majority of the people of Bengal. The genius of the Indian peasantry has not yet been able to discover the advantages of rotation of crops which, since its adoption in England, has been productive of so much good. The plough employed in our country is of the simplest sort,—perhaps the extreme fertility of the soil does not require a better one,—and no means have yet been adopted to provide against drought or excessive fall of rain, which almost periodically causes so much scarcity and misery among the poor people. It is unfortunate that rice, which is the main food of the people of Bengal, should, more than perhaps any other crop, be dependant on the periodical rains. Contingencies will happen; and an extensive system of irrigation, which alone can provide against such contingencies, requires an amount of energy and co-operation which does not exist among our peasants, and which, we may add, cannot exist among any class of peasantry so poor and withal so situated as the peasantry of India.

Women in villages are allowed a greater degree of liberty than their sisters in towns. There is no objection to their going about from place to place, to fetch water from the tank, or to go and bathe in the river; but except in the case of elderly widows or women verging on old age, they are not permitted to speak with people other than the younger members of their own family. Drunkenness is almost unknown in our villages; and cases of cruelty to wives are also rare; and in both these respects the lowest classes of people in our country are superior to the same classes of people in more civilized countries. Wives, too, are, generally speaking, affectionate and faithful to their husbands, and family peace is maintained in the villages to a remarkable extent.

As in towns girls are married at an early age in villages, but generally speaking they remain with their mothers, even after marriage, till they attain their youth. The ceremony of marriage consists of a variety of little and often puerile rites which represent the bestowal of the bride to the bridegroom who on that occasion makes a present to the parents of the girl. This last rite, which in some shape or other seems to obtain among all tribes and nations, points to a period in the history of man when daughters were considered to be the property of their parents and were *sold* to the bridegroom; and this *sale* with the advance of civilization has transformed itself into marriage. In her husband's house the ryot's wife always makes herself useful. She cleans huts and compounds, prepares meals for her husband, cleans utensils, husks grains all round the year in the *dheki*, fetches water from neighbouring tanks and ghats, prepares lamps, looks to the cows and her children, and is busy all the day long. After her morning duties are done, she goes to the tank or to the river-side to bathe, and about noon every village ghat may be seen crowded with women loitering sometimes for hours together with their never-ending gossip and scandal.

We have said, the ryot's wife is, generally speaking, faithful to her husband; but exceptions not unfrequently occur. In the villages, where only a handful of people live together and where every one knows what his neighbour does, female frailty is seldom long a secret. Husbands however are sometimes found to live with their wives who are known to be frail in character, and women who have probably eloped once or twice are also sometimes taken back by their husbands,—a thing which could never happen among the higher class people.

Young widows seldom remain pure in character. A solitary life is felt to be so cheerless, the temptations are so strong, that they are seldom resisted. In most cases the young widow elopes with some particular villager, and then remains constant to him for probably years together as his wife to all intents and purposes. When we consider that widow marriage is strictly interdicted by the Hindu religion, when we think of the extreme hardship which a widow has to put up with specially if she is an orphan, we are almost tempted to excuse her conduct when she flies from her distress to the protection of a man,—we are almost inclined to admire her constancy and faith towards her chosen paramour, for so society calls him. Prostitution as it obtains in our towns is unknown in villages.

With Mahommedans the state of things is slightly different. It is allowable for a Mahommedan widow to marry again, and in such instances the simple *Nika* system of marriage is generally adopted as distinguished from the more important and cumbrous rites of the *Shadi* ceremony. In the eye of law and religion the *Nika* is valid marriage, but in practice it is often nothing more or less than concubinage. If a vagabond deserts his old and faithful wife and takes to a young widow, there is a *Nika* between them, and the new wife is as much a wife in the eye of the law as the old. Divorce which is unknown among Hindus is as simple among Mahommedans as the *Nika* system of marriage, and cases are by no means uncommon in which a young wife divorced by her husband by a single word of mouth goes off, contracts *Nika* with another man by another word of mouth, and is *his* wife; and men and women may be found who have contracted *Nikas* several times in their lives. In some respects however the Mahommedan system is better than the Hindu;—a Mahommedan widow, who takes to a new man and is constant to him, is and ought to be considered his wife by *Nika*, while a Hindu woman under the same circumstances is most unjustly branded as a paramour. As we have said before, these irregularities (except in the case of young widows) are not frequent, and except when the husband is a fool and a vagabond, or when the wife is of a notoriously dissolute character, family peace and connubial faithfulness prevail in village homes.

The ryot is still as primitive a creature as he was centuries ago. A somewhat long *sari* wound round the body serves as the clothing of the ryot's wife, a scantier piece of cloth, extending from the waist to the knee, and often a second bit of cloth thrown on the shoulders serves for the ryot himself. The home of the ryot generally consists of one or two huts built on raised mud platforms, and always kept exceedingly clean by the women. Well-to-do ryots have one or two huts more. Cows are kept in a small cow-shed, and *dheki* or the husking machine is neatly planted beside the huts and is found to be constantly at work. Mats generally serve as beds for the ryots, the *tuktoposh* being used only by a few of the well-to-do peasants. A few brass utensils,—some dhan stored in earthen jars, a plough, the brass or silver ornaments of the women, occasionally a spinning wheel, and sometimes a few kids, these added to what have been mentioned before would form a pretty complete inventory of the ryot's property.

The ryot's main property,—the means of his livelihood, the ground of all his hopes,—the scope of all his ambition, is the little bit of land he cultivates;—and it is easy to imagine he is passionately fond of it. Western notions of comforts and conveniences of life have availed the ryot but little,—the luxuries of a civilized life he does not aspire to, of wealth he has none, education he seeks not. He has one and but one thing to compensate for all his wants,—his land and his annual crops. His most dearly cherished hope points to nothing higher than a good harvest; his greatest fear is lest his produce is decreased or his rent increased. He does anything and everything to produce a good harvest. He ploughs his land over and over, he sows with care, he weeds the infant plants repeatedly with almost parental affection, and when the corn is nearly ripe he often passes entire nights in the fields, always watching and sleepless lest trespassing cattle do any injury to his crops. Is it a matter of wonder, then, that he should be passionately fond of his little bit of land,—that he should jealously guard his interests in his land? Abuse him, and the ryot will not complain; beat him and he will but bend; but increase the rent, and he can bear no more,—the last straw breaks the camel's back. It is this class of oppressions that he feels most cruelly and reflects upon most bitterly.

During the sowing and reaping seasons the ryots are busy in the fields all the day long. Early in the morning they take a meal and go to the fields. There they work till about noon. In such seasons women often take rice to their husbands working in the fields at noon. After this meal, the ryots lay themselves down under some trees and repose for a while, and labor again till evening, when they return with weary limbs and weary cattle to their homes to take a third meal which their wives have prepared against their coming.

The gorgeous mythology of Hinduism has never been unfolded to these ignorant people, and their religion mainly consists in a variety of little ceremonies performed in the different seasons of the year. The gods too whom they worship are of a specially agrarian character, and such as are expected to supply the wants and avert the dangers incident to village life. Death from snake-bite is a most frequent occurrence in the villages, and the *Mansha* plant is worshipped as a remedy. *Makal* Thakur is supposed to give an abundance of fish all round the year, and receives worship from boatmen and fishermen, and *Shashti* who is supposed to bestow children, and *Panchanan* who keeps them in good health, are universally worshipped. The Mahommedan villagers stick to their comparatively refined religion, and in purely Mahommedan villages there is almost always a place of worship where people assemble on Fridays, and prayers are loudly chanted to God and to Mahomet. Descendants as they undoubtedly are of the Hindus of olden days, the agricultural Mahommedans of Bengal still retain the habits and manners of the Hindu population of the country. In some few respects however marked differences are observable. Mahommedan women, for instance, are kept in closer seclusion even in villages than the Hindu, and in religious matters the Mahommedans are generally speaking more strict in their faith and practices.

It is thus interesting to go through a large village and observe the various sections of the community, differing from each other by slight shades only, and all remaining in peace and harmony with each other. First then there is the Mahommedan *párá* or portion of village where women are kept in a somewhat close seclusion, and where the inhabitants perform their own religious rites and regularly assemble to chant their Friday prayers. Then there is the Hindu *párá* where the inhabitants, let us suppose, are mostly *Kaibartas* by caste who have not much to do with religion except as it is represented in small rites and ceremonies. Then there is probably a *párá* for the *Mals*, fishermen and boatmen, who ply boats sometimes for hire, but mostly for fishing purposes. They fill every *beel* and river with nets and *Bandals*, and long before night has waned go in bodies to capture fish. Sometimes they take torches with them which are supposed to bring up the fish to the surface of the water. They are good divers, worship *Makal* Thakur, and carry on a profitable trade for which they pay something to the zemindars who hold *jalkar* in the river or *beel* in question. Then, again, there is probably a *párá* for the Domes, Muchies and Haris, people of the lowest class, who live in the dirtiest part of the village, surrounded by their flocks of pigs and weaving mats which bring them a tolerably good income.

We might also divide the population according to the position they occupy. First of all come in the Gomashta and his myrmidons who form the head of the village in power, prestige and importance. Scarcely less important is the village Mohajan with his golas of dhan. To him the cultivators look up for dhan all the year round. He lends them dhan for themselves and their families, he lends them money to pay the zemindar's rent, and he also helps them to buy clothing, utensils and other simple necessaries of village life, and to employ laborers in their fields in the weeding season. And the whole annual debt is paid up at the annual harvest. Next come in the village notables, the few Mondals who know how to read and write and to whom the villagers look up as the men of learning,—the putwari if there is any such in the village,—the chowkidar who keeps watch in the village by strolling through it in the night with loud cries to intimidate thieves and give assurance to honest people; and the village smith and carpenter to whom every body comes to have their ploughs made. Next to these come in the respectable villagers who hold land more or less in quantity in the fields surrounding the villages, and who have all their accounts with the Mohajan. Last come in the laborers who have no lands of their own, but help the other villagers in the field in the sowing and reaping seasons, help them in building up huts or excavating pools, and in the winter season crowd to the Bádá to reap the superb harvest of that part of the country. Generally speaking they get no loan of the Mohajans, but get dhan or money from those who employ them, and thus live by their daily labor.

We have seen that the Hindu villagers at least have not much of religion, and yet caste quarrels, called *daladali* fill our villages. If a wife who has once eloped is taken back by her husband, he and his family are outcasted, if a frail widow finds a shelter in her father's house, that father is out-casted. Caste quarrels mostly take root in such occurrences, but are often made a handmaid to land disputes which, it may easily be supposed, often rage fiercely among a people with whom land is the only property. Entire villages are sometimes divided into parties, each claiming a particular bit of land to be its own, and feuds and rioting are by no means uncommon in the sowing and reaping seasons.

Panchyets, which at one time had great influence in our villages, are still sometimes called to heal these disputes, but their influence is decreasing day by day. At a time when there was little chance of villagers obtaining justice anywhere, an indigenous system arose and was developed as it were by the very necessity of having all disputes settled at home. That necessity does not any longer exist, as under the British administration in Bengal justice is almost brought to every poor man's door; and Panchyets too are gradually losing their power and prestige, and every ryot has learnt to look on the Court of Justice as the place where his fate will ultimately be decided.

We might again divide the peasantry who hold land under zemindars or taluqdars according to the nature of the holding. First comes the patnidar, generally a man of considerable substance and holding land on fixed rent under the zemindar. It is not in every village that a patnidar is to be found. The patnidar often sublets land to the durpatnidar, who may sublet to the sepatnidar, and so on to the fourth or fifth degree. Next to the patnidar in importance and rank are the istemrardars and mukarraridars who are often called mourusi gantidars. The difference that exists between these three is very slight and often only nominal. They also hold land on fixed rent and are generally men of considerable substance. Like a patni, a ganti is hereditary and transferable, and the rent payable is not liable to enhancement. Gantis may also be held for a stated period of time, in which case they resemble leases or izaras in respect of the rights conferred.

The izaradar holds under the zemindar or taluqdar and sublets to the ryots, keeping a margin of rent for himself for his trouble and risk in collection. This tenure is generally unpopular with ryots, as the izaradar always anxious to widen the margin aforesaid is often more harassing to the ryots than the zemindars would have been had they taken rent direct from the ryots. The izara is again sublet to dur-izaradars and se-izaradars. The rent of land has so much increased since the Permanent Settlement that a host of outsiders have come in to share the profits which Lord Cornwallis reserved for the zemindars alone.

We may here speak of the holders of revenue-free estates. Revenue-free estates were created by grants from the Mahommedan sovereigns for service done, or by Rajas to Brahmans, priests and Vaishnavas, or consecrated for the worship of Hindu idols or Mahommedan *pirs* or saints. Small bits of such lands are now held rent-free by respectable villagers; and it is the constant aim of many zemindars to somehow incorporate such lands within their lands thereby getting rent from lands for which no rent is payable.

Last come in the ryots, properly so called, who have been divided into three classes by Act X. of 1859 as elsewhere specified. The *utbandi* ryots, those who have no permanent rights to the land, are the most numerous, and they are entirely at the mercy of the zemindars. This brings us to one of the most important questions of the day, namely the relation in the present day between the ryots and the zemindars.

There are some who would have us believe that the peasantry of Bengal are to the present day the same helpless and oppressed race that they were centuries ago,—that the zemindars of the present day have still as free a scope for oppression as they had before. Wrongful confinement, extortion, and oppression of the most fearful description, still prevail, according to them, through the length and breadth of the country, and the ryots, who are saints in their suffering and quite ignorant of any way in which redress may be obtained against the all-powerful zemindar and his myrmidons, suffer in silence. Thanks to the enlightened principles of the British Government, this picture represents a state of things which exists not in the present day.

There is another class of writers numbering unfortunately in their ranks some of the most influential editors, associations, and members of the Hindu community who would represent the zemindars as the martyrs of the day. According to them, ryots everywhere know their rights, and wilfully and maliciously withhold rent, and so torment their zemindars without the least cause or provocation. Much talent and influence are exerted to support this view,—but the highest talent and greatest influence will fail when consciously exerted in the cause of a lie.

To one who has lived for any length of time in the Mofussil the real state of things cannot be unknown. The chain of absolute servitude have been rent asunder by a liberal Government, but the zemindar still possesses a variety of means to harass the ryots, and these means are not unfrequently exerted. There is probably not a single zemindari in Bengal in which more is not taken from the ryots in some shape or other than is due by law; in which the Naib, the Gomasta, &c., do not make illegal extortions from the ryot. In at least ninety per cent. of the zemindaris abwabs are still freely collected from the ryots on such occasions as the birth of a zemindar's son or the marriage of a zemindar's daughter; and we are assured by respectable zemindars that these abwabs are freely and sometimes cheerfully given by the ryots on such occasions. And the risk and danger of falling out with a zemindar is so great that there is scarcely a single zemindari where the ryots would not willingly pay somewhat more than is due rather than combine against their zemindars. We have the very best authority for stating, and we state the fact emphatically, that ryots will not turn against their masters till the latter first turn cruelly oppressive. But our experience is limited, and our very best authority would probably be considered of little weight. Well then we have it from some really good and respectable zemindars themselves, that ryots will never combine against their zemindars till brought to straits. On the contrary, instances are by no means uncommon,—and may be cited by dozens by those who live in the Mofussil—of ryots voluntarily giving six months' or a year's rent in advance to save the estate of a really kind master. And indeed this stands to reason. The risk which a ryot runs of being harassed and ultimately ruined, if he comes to terms of disagreement with his master, is so great, that he makes it a point never to fall out with him so long as it can be helped; and when estates are going off from the hands of a really kind master, the chances that his successor will prove equally kind and see every thing with his own eyes and not through subordinates, who almost invariably turn out little tyrants, are so slight, that the ryot spares no pains, no sacrifices to keep a really good master in his place. Wherefore, then, the impression that the ryots in the present day are most to blame for the rent disputes prevailing all over the country? We answer, the impression is totally false, and there are ample reasons to account for such a false impression. Public opinion in this country means the opinion of the aristocracy and middle classes,—in one word, the opinion of the *Bhadralok* and not of the cultivating and working classes ;—and there are ample reasons why such a public opinion should be strongly biased in favor of the zemindars. In villages the *Bhadralok* is in nine cases out of ten either himself a zemindar in a large or a small scale, or belongs to a zemindar's family. In towns, the most influential of the *Bhadralok*,—the aristocracy,—the millionaries,—the enlightened,—those who create an opinion and not receive it from others, are almost all zemindars. The most powerful association is an association of the zemindars,—the most influential newspaper is an organ of the zemindars. Is it a wonder then that public opinion throughout this vast country should be regularly blind to the faults of our landed aristocracy?—that every act of shame should be laid at the door of the voiceless and unrepresented ryot? Poor Bengal Ryot! Hope for relief from a hand of alien rulers of the country,—but from thine own countrymen,—Don't. There is also another reason to account for the generally unfavorable impression against the ryot. The people of Bengal are pre-eminently a conservative one, and implicitly follow the maxim, whatever is, is right. We have seen elsewhere that under the Mahommedan rulers of Bengal the cultivating classes were placed in complete servitude under the zemindars,—and their happiness and comfort depended on the will and pleasure of their masters. Such a state, then, is assumed by our countrymen as the normal state of society,—and every step bringing about the independence of the ryot is considered to be a step towards anarchy!

And yet it were idle to deny that the differences and disputes between zemindars and ryots are daily assuming a serious aspect. We are aware that the combining of the ryots *en masse* against their zemindars is at the present day no rare occurrence, that in some instances ryots have been betrayed to acts of indiscretion. Those who advocate the cause of our zemindars point to these facts as convincing arguments to prove the iniquity of the ryots. We shall therefore dwell at some length on these occurrences.

The rising of the people *en masse* in an entire district is certainly a singular phenomenon among a peasantry so mild as that of Bengal. We have had risings of chiefs, risings of sects, risings of fanatics, risings of insurgents in this country; but of risings of a purely agricultural character we have had but few instances in olden times. And yet within the last twenty years we have had two instances of this sort, *viz.*, the indigo disturbance of Nuddea, and the late rent disturbance of Pubna. Perhaps it will not be a bootless task to enquire into the causes of these risings under the British Government. At the risk of being put down as paradoxical and perverse in our opinions, we shall venture to assert, that we see in them a good sign of the times;—that we find in them some evidence that the moral of a civilized mode of administration has not been entirely lost on the millions of Bengal. The British Government with its correct principles of equality, and its resolute curbing of oppression wherever and whenever found, has already freed the peasantry of Bengal from that galling servitude of thought and action in which they remained enchained for centuries, and which rendered action on their part impossible; it has already inspired them with confidence, and given them a degree of assurance which they never knew before. For centuries together the peasantry remained in complete servitude under the zemindars of Bengal. Those who are familiar with the details of administration in Bengal in the last days of Mahommedan rule unanimously admit, that the zemindars of those days were the supreme rulers of the people under them; they were indeed little feudatory chiefs bound only to pay revenue to the subadar. Their internal administration was never interfered with, and when they chose to be oppressive, against their oppression there was no redress. Under such circumstances it was not a matter of surprize to find the peasantry devoid of all energy—of all hope of resistance. At a time when resistance was certain to prove futile, action became impossible, combination was folly, silent servitude was natural, and grew into a fixed habit. We confess we are pleased to find evidences that the millions of Bengal are at last awakening from this lethargy, and that, retaining the peaceful habits of their forefathers, they are yet in the present day capable of action in cases of emergency. And we believe we are stating a simple truth when we say, that the development of this healthy feature in the character of the Bengal ryot is entirely due to the policy of the British Government in Bengal which recognizes no class of oppressors under its shadow.

The advocates of the zemindars ascribe this change to the self-same cause, but entirely misrepresent or fail to understand its character. They agree with us in saying that open resistance on the part of the ryots did not exist before, but while we view with complaisance the development of this feature in the ryot's character, they regret it as a mark of hostility between the zemindar and the ryot which has been fostered by the British Government. Who taught the ryot, they ask, to rush to the civil court on the least disagreement with his zemindar? Who taught him to haul his master, the Gomasta or the Naib, in the criminal court for the pettiest act of oppression? It is the British Government with its Penal Code, and its Act X. of 1859. Before these enactments there was no hostility between the zemindar and the royt; every thing (in their words) was calm and still.

Perhaps it was so; but it was the stillness of the desert and the calm of death! There was no open hostility, because hostility was action, and action was impossible. Servitude, silent, unmurmuring, voiceless, servitude was the order of the day,—and the order was well kept. Oppression called forth no resistance, tyranny evoked no groan! The guilt, the crime of the British Government has been in affording the ryot a means of publishing, perhaps of opposing gross oppression,—and this has offended our zemindars, our press, our so-called public opinion! Yes,—there has been an awakening of the peasantry from a long sleep of servitude, and we shall venture to assert that we for one view it with complaisance. It evidences a real hankering of the masses after improvement, and such hankering in independent countries has always been the parent of national rights and liberties. The crisis is come, and some decisive action on the part of the Government is absolutely necessary. Chaos or confusion is not the normal state of nature or society,—the commotion at present observable will not last for ever,—it must settle down one way or another, and it depends on the Government in what way it settles down. Two ways are now open to Government. To put down the general awakening and to leave the ryots once more at the mercy of the zemindar, as has been done times without number from 1793 to 1859;

or to take a more enlightened and intelligent view of the general rising, and to newly create, in a more satisfactory manner than has yet been done, a definite status of the ryot and a definite status of the zemindar.

The first step would be, to say the least, illiberal and short-sighted. The "yeomanry of Bengal" have already many and tangible grounds of complaint against the British Grovernment. English legislation has already much to answer for. We need not repeat here what we have pointed out elsewhere, *viz.*, the serious mistakes of British legislation committed ever since the memorable year 1793 ;—but we venture to hope for the sake of the masses of the people of Bengal that such mistakes will not be repeated again.

We have said that to settle the question finally by putting down the rising with a strong hand would be *illiberal* and *unjust.* If such arguments will not prevail with our rulers we shall say more ; and shew that to settle the question *finally* in that way is *impossible.* The question cannot be settled that way; the problem does not admit of such a solution. Such a step would be a tiding over present difficulties to be sure,—but it would not be a permanent solution of it, as the same difficulties will in that case rise again 5 or 10 years hence and stare rudely at our face demanding further solution. And wherefore? The answer is to be sought for in the spirit of English administration in India. The noble instincts of every Englishman are against the servitude of one class under another, and so long as Englishmen are the masters of this country that servitude can never be made permanent. The legislation of Lord Cornwallis may have ignored the rights of the peasantry,—the legislation of Lord Wellesley may have subjected them and their property to the tender mercies of the zemindars,—the legislation of after years may have perpetrated acts of deeper shame,—but all, all is useless. Every individual Englishman, called upon to administer the country, cannot but sympathise with the ryot maltreated and ejected by his zemindar,—notwithstanding that such ejection may be sanctified by the law of the land,—and it is this sympathy that gives the ryot confidence and assurance in spite of masses of legislation. If our rulers could regard the happiness of the mass of the people as a subordinate consideration or no consideration at all, if they could as complacently look on the servitude of one class under another (so long as the revenue was safe) as the Mahommedan rulers did, then they might have once for all settled all questions between the zemindar and the ryot by permanently ignoring all rights of the latter, and the peasantry might once more have sunk down to that voiceless servitude whence they have risen. But no; the better instincts of a free nation revolt against such a solution; and, as we have said, it is those very instincts manifesting themselves in the daily and hourly administration of the country that have taught the peasantry to awake from their long sleep, despite perverse and mistaken acts of legislation which contemplated the stamping out of all spirit and energy from a down-trodden race of cultivators. And if the general awakening at the present moment be put down once more with a strong hand and by mistaken legislation, those very English instincts will in a future day cause a fresh rising of the masses,—and the problem will rise again and again demanding a permanent and intelligent solution.

There is then one and only one way left before the Government ;—to estimate the importance of the general rising correctly,—to grapple with the problem intelligently,—to newly create the status of the zemindar and the ryot in a definite manner,—to enact a PERMANENT SETTLEMENT between the zemindar and the ryot as a Permanent Settlement has been enacted between the zemindars and the Government.

In the face of the crisis that is staring rudely at us, half-hearted legislation would be useless and worse than useless. Our rulers will not, cannot once more *degrade* the ryot to his pristine position of servitude under the zemindars,—the only other measure then to heal the ill feeling between the two classes, and to put a stop to the mass of litigation that is eating into the very vitals of an agricultural population is to *raise* the status of the ryots. *Let the rates of rent now payable be carefully ascertained after an extensive survey, and let such rates be declared fixed for ever.*

This would be a bold step, but we believe it would be one truly beneficial to the country. We know such an arrangement would disturb a nest of hornets, but the Government of India has before now shown itself capable of boldly serving the country in spite of masses of selfishness and class interests that may block the way. We are stating our simple conviction that we cannot think of one valid reason that may be brought forward against this sort of arrangement.

It would be loudly and vehemently urged that such an Act would be a breach of the promise of 1793—an invasion of the rights of the zemindars. To this objection we would answer,—nowhere in the Permanent Settlement is it stated that Government should never set a limit to the demands of the zemindars on the cultivating classes. On the contrary, Section VIII. of Act I. of 1793 distinctly declares, that the Governor-General would in future be competent to enact any regulations that may be considered proper for the protection of the ryots; and now that the revenue of every zemindari has increased two or three-fold, and the ryots have been harassed for scores of years with ever-increasing claims on the part of the zemindars, the time is surely come when some assurance of a definite nature should be given to the ryots against the all-devouring claims of the zemindar;—when the ryot in his turn should be promised the future increase of the revenue of land. No one in the present day would be foolhardy enough to suppose that Lord Canning's Act X of 1859 was a violation of the promise made to zemindars in 1793. And yet Lord Canning let a definite limit to the claims of the zemindars with respect to certain classes of ryots; and how the extension of the same protection to all ryots can be a violation of the Permanent settlement we entirely fail to see.

The fact is, the Permanent Settlement simply defined the relation between the zemindars and the Government, and left the subject of the relation between the zemindar and the ryot open for later legislation. Later legislation, accordingly, has taken up the subject,—we have seen at one time the persons and properties of the ryots subjected to the tender mercies of the zemindar, and we have seen at another time the ryots declared to possess no rights whatever. All these were changed again, and Lord Canning invested the ryots with some rights. The whole history of British legislature in Bengal clearly proves that no definite promise was ever made to the zemindar regarding the degree of power he might exercise on the ryot. Legislation has before now set limits to the rights of the zemindar, and if at the present day it be deemed politic to set a still more definite limit on the powers of the zemindar, Sec. VIII. of Act I. of 1793 distinctly allows it and nothing on earth prevents it.

And if the measure is perfectly lawful, it is no less expedient. A few enlightened zemindars of Calcutta have from time to time represented some of the grievances of the people, but those who would believe that these zemindars *represent* in any sense of the word the ordinary village zemindar would commit a sad mistake. Without an iota of education or public spirit or desire to do good to the people, the typical village zemindar considers it the aim and object of his life to extort the last penny from the impoverished ryot. In this calamitous year, when the Government of India and the Government of Bengal tried head and heart to save millions from starvation—when even in provinces where scarcity did not appear, liberal loans were granted by Government to keep the people from harm, what did our zemindars do? A few enlightened zemindars remitted or promised to remit a portion of the rent due, and our newspapers are never tired singing their praises *ad nauseam*; but when we turn our eyes from the newspapers to the country that stretches on all sides of us, what do we see? Self-seeking and selfishness, a cruel disregard for the sufferings of the ryots, a most startling unconsciousness of the moral duty imposed on every one at this terrible season,—these characterize the masses of the zemindars. Nay more. Not twenty miles from where we are writing, a rich and heartless zemindar has been for the last several years harassing his ryots in the cruellest manner for increase of rent. Some of the ryots have left the country,—others are imprisoned,—all have been ruined and impoverished. And this calamitous year has been chosen as a fitting occasion to heap fresh cruelties on the heads of the ryots and thus bring them back to their accustomed servitude! Is this an isolated instance? Are our experiences singular on this point? We ask others who form their opinions from actual facts, and not from newspapers, and the same dismal story is repeated. And yet, who is this zemindar, who harasses the ryots for increase of rent? *He* sits quietly at his comfortable house in the city of palaces,—*they* labor in the field from sunrise to sunset and often keep vigils from sunset to sunrise; *they* work under the burning sun of May, under the torrents of August and in the shivering cold of December; *they* till the land and sow it, and weed the plants and reap the corn,—and *they* are harassed because they are unwilling to part with an ever-increasing portion of the fruits of their unceasing work. What is it that thus enables the zemindar to harass these ryots? Is there any moral right which enables an idler to oppress the poor and the lowly? The code of morals must be strange, indeed, which would sanctify such a deed. Is it that the zemindars are powerful and are so enabled to harass the weak? Those days are gone by, and under the shadow of the British lion the strong man trembles and the weak gets assurance and hope. No, it is a mistaken legislation which thus allows even to the present day a chronic oppression of the peasantry,—a legislation which it would not be a day too soon to mend.

The only other seemingly valid objection that suggests itself to us is, that the measure proposed will not ultimately tend to the good of the cultivators. It will be urged that, as the revenue of the land is constantly increasing, the cultivators, called upon to pay a fixed rent in future, will in the course of time be enabled to sublet their lands, will in a manner form a sort of permanent izardars, and paying the fixed rent to the zemindar will be enabled to exact much more from those who will then actually cultivate the soil. It will be thus plausibly argued that the measure aforesaid will in the long run only create a prosperous class of harassing izárdárs,—that the cultivators of the land 50 years hence will be just as badly off as the cultivators of the present day. All this however may be avoided by the law distinctly stating that so much and no more will be exacted for ever in future,—not from the present cultivators and their inheritors and descendants,—but from those who in the present time or in future times may actually cultivate the land.

We shall here recapitulate. Two ways are open before Government, *viz.*, to allow the ryots to sink once more into complete obedience and servitude under zemindars, or to raise the status of the ryots by setting a definite limit to the claims of the zemindar. The first has the sanction of immemorial usage, and it will be pertinently asked why it should be changed for the latter. It will be boldly asserted that the complete dependence of the ryot on the zemindar will heal all differences, and will in the end be really conducive to the well-being of the peasantry. Wherefore, then, do we advocate the raising of the status of the agricultural classes by setting definite limits to the claims of the zemindars ?

We answer,—for several reasons.

Firstly.—So long as the claims of the zemindars are allowed to be unlimited, ryots can *never* be expected to be prudent, provident, thinking beings. As matters stand now, if a ryot dares to save anything, the zemindar is certain by hook or by crook to ease him of his savings. The ryot therefore revenges himself on his oppressors by never saving anything, by living and working on borrowed capital all the year round. Is it desirable that the ryot should ever be a provident, thinking being? Assure him that his savings are his own, that permanent limits have been set to the claims of the zemindar, and the strong motive of self-interest will alter the custom of long centuries.

Secondly.—Candour and truthfulness are the attributes of independence. Mendacity, falsehood and cunning accompany rigid subjection. In how many criminal or civil cases will the ryot of the present day dare to swear to a fact against the interest of his zemindar?—in how many thousands of instances is he taught to perjure himself for his zemindar, to merge all fear of God and of man in his fear for his master? We as a nation have often been branded for cunning and falsehood; is the day not yet come when the institutions which perpetuate those vices should be one by one disestablished?

The comparative freedom in thought and action, secured to the higher classes by an enlightened Government, have already produced wonderful results; and the officials of the present day selected from our educated classes will not compare unfavorably, for honesty and truthfulness, with the Europeans of the country, and will present a marked contrast to the same class of people living a century ago. Is it desirable to instil the same truthfulness and honesty into the cultivating classes? Remove the pains and penalties under which they have for centuries together been compelled to learn cunning,—set limits to the now unlimited powers of the zemindar, and *some* change for the better will of certainty be observable, though the vices of a century are not cured in a day.

Thirdly.—Independence begets the will and the power to resist, servitude smothers them altogether. We have heard much of the extortions of the Police, the zemindars, the planters and the tax-gatherers. And yet in no country has Government so strenuously exerted itself to put a stop to such extortions as in Bengal. How is it then, it may be asked, that they exist to the present day? The answer lies in a nutshell. In a country where the people are so utterly void of the power of resistance that the constable and the planter's underling can get out something for the mere asking,—all legislation to put a stop to such practices will fail. The ryot's property is not more zealously guarded in England than it is in Bengal,—but the English tax-gatherer fears,—

not so much the jealousy of the law, but the power of village Hampdens protesting against the least approach to extortion. We do not expect that Hampdens with dauntless breasts will rise in our villages as soon as a limit is set to zemindars' powers,—but we do expect that a comparative independence will awaken (as to a certain extent it has already done) some spirit of resistance; and that will be a better safeguard of the ryot's property than any amount of legislation.

Fourthly.—An expectation was entertained by the framers of the Permanent Settlement that that measure would induce the zemindars to improve their possessions. The Act however has not only brought about no such improvement, but has actually precluded the possibility of such improvement. The zemindars themselves have been grossly negligent in the performance of such duties. And as for the ryot,—wherefore should he improve his bit of land? Wherefore should he bring about any improvement by *his* labor and outlay which in the end is sure to benefit his master. A very large proportion indeed of the ryots are *utbandi*, or tenants at will, and should they bring about such improvement, the law distinctly empowers their master to rob them of the fruits of their labor by increasing rent or turning them out of the land after the improvement has been completed. A small portion of the cultivators are occupancy ryots, and even they, though empowered by law to enjoy the fruits of any improvement they may bring about, will find it difficult to hold their own against masses of evidence which the zemindar can at any moment fabricate and bring forward at a court of justice to prove, either that the ryot has not the right of occupancy or that he has not effected the improvement. But declare that all ryots have rights of occupancy,—and are entitled to every increase in the productive powers of lands that may henceforth accrue, and a stimulus will be afforded for effecting improvements which even Asiatic indolence will scarcely resist.

We need not dwell any longer on this subject. The candid reader will not fail to conceive a variety of ways in which the ryots will be benefited if some sort of assurance and security, such as has been indicated above, were afforded to them. Such readers will not require any arguments from us to be convinced of the difference between a state of subjection and almost servitude, and one of comparative independence. To him we have said enough, but to others, who will persist in maintaining a state of dependence on zemindars to be the most happy one for ryots, any thing that we can ever urge, will be urged in vain.

We are no theoretical reformers. We do not consider a *Permanent Settlement* between the ryots and zemindars as a panacea to all evils that the ryot's flesh is heir to. We do not consider it possible for legislation to bring about any sudden change in the character of a nation. But we do think there are several ways in which such a measure will tend to improve the character and condition of the people, and, entertaining such notions, we should have been wanting in our duty if we did not advocate the measure.

To sum up in a few words:—the measure aforesaid will bestow strong motives for improving land on those by whom alone land has been improved in every country; it will put a stop to the mass of harrassing litigation which is doing indescribable evil to the country and of which we shall speak in the next chapter; it will elevate the millions of Bengal to a status which they fully deserve but never occupied before; it will develop in the character of the ryot such virtues as independence and self-reliance, prudence and economy for the first time in the history of Bengal; it will for ever put a stop to zemindari extortions and oppression which, in spite of the good will and the vigour of English administration, have not ceased to the present day; it will bestow the fruits of labor not on a class of enervated idlers but on those who toil and sweat and hold the plough; it will bestow the blessings of the British rule on the million and not on the upper ten thousand; and it will reflect eternal glory on the crown of England.*

* The zemindari interest in the land is strong, and it is possible all we have said has been said in vain. The day is probably yet distant when the claims of the zemindar shall be permanently fixed. If so, we appeal to our rulers if the time is not yet come when some limit of some sort or other should be set on the power of the zemindar to increase rent and oust ryots who have not rights of possession. The evil is a crying one, and demands immediate redress.

CHAPTER V.

ADMINISTRATION OF JUSTICE.

> But that name shall be restored,
> Law and justice wield her sword,
> And her God shall be adored.
>
> MONTGOMERY.

FEW people will, we believe, in the present day, be inclined to dispute the fact, that justice is now much better administered in this country than under the best of the Mahommedan rulers. If the rich have still an advantage over the poor, such advantage we hope is decreasing every day; and legislation, it must be admitted, is trying hard to help those who cannot help themselves. The equality on principle of all men is unhesitatingly recognized by our courts, and though we have not yet seen this principle carried into action, the recognition of the principle itself is a great thing;—it is so much gained in the cause of humanity.

Antecedent to the coming of the English to this country, a portion of the judicial work seems to have been performed by the *kázis* who were versed in Mahommedan literature and expounded the Mahommedan law. A large portion of the criminal work however came before the governor or other executive officer of the province, while petty cases among the poor people in the country parts were mostly decided by the zemindars living on the spot; and this practice still continues to some extent all over the country. It cannot be denied that substantial justice was done in most cases by this system of administration, as the parties who sat in judgment could hardly fail to ascertain the real facts in any particular case, and were indeed in many cases personally acquainted with the true facts. Such courts, however, as may be expected, were open to corruption, and there was little chance of justice being done therefore, when the proud man oppressed the poor and the lowly.

Nor should we forget to mention the village Panchayets of Bengal, which were among the most beautiful and beneficial institutions of the land. The Panchayet consisted of the most respectable men in the village, and as the members were hardly ever ignorant of the real facts of the case, the most arduous duty of a judge was simplified, and there was little temptation for falsehood or concealment of the truth. The Panchayet sat surrounded by the good and *mátabbar* men of the village, and, after discussing in a conversational style the facts of the case, pronounced their judgment in the presence of all. This way of settling disputes is by no means bad, and it is a pity the practice is fast falling off. At the same time, however, it must be remembered, that Panchayets will answer only in petty cases, and cannot be expected to do justice in cases in which one of the parties is strong or influential. Even in petty cases, we need assurance that the Panchayets did not betray a weakness for men of superior caste, or men endued with exceptional claims to deference and respect.

Such, then, was in short the system of administration of justice among our forefathers, and few will deny that it was vastly inferior to the system at present obtaining. Corruption was the bane of the system under the Mahommedans, corruption is unheard of among the judicial officers of the present day. In a word, the Mahommedan system facilitated the work of ascertaining the real facts of any particular case, but left the gates of corruption wide open; the English system secured integrity but threw obstacles in the way of ascertaining the truth. The English on coming to this country declared, and rightly declared, that corruption was the greater evil of the two, and doomed and discarded the old system, and introduced the English system in India. To shew how far it is possible to combine the two systems and choose a happy medium, and to point out the defects of the system now obtaining, are the purposes of this chapter.

We have said that our rulers introduced the English system into India. Unfortunately they introduced it almost word per word and letter per letter;—they forgot to modify it in accordance with the peculiar wants and exigencies of the country. The main defects, therefore, in the administration of justice in this country, are such as a foreign nation may be expected to commit through its inability to realize the peculiar requirements of a different people. Judicial maxims and institutions, which have grown up among the people of England during centuries together, have been transferred almost bodily to India. It seems to have never been considered that, in every country, there are a thousand and one different conditions which, like the minute wheels of an engine, regulate and modify the action of any particular maxim or institution, and that these conditions are widely different in India from what they are in England.

One of the most prominent instances, in which an English institution has miserably failed in its working in this country, will be found in the system of jury trial. Even in England, it is by no means unusual to hear in the present day the advisability of continuing jury trials called into question, and the arguments brought forward are often not easy to refute. English juries of olden times, - times when the liberties of the people were threatened by the whims of oppressive kings and oppressive courts,—did invaluable service by saving the lives and properties of the people. In times, too, when the corruption of English judges was as notorious as their integrity is in the present times, the jury system was a safe-guard against injustice by precluding the possibility of corruption. But these and such like reasons in favor of jury trials have now ceased to exist. Oppression of kings and royal courts is in the present day impossible in England, as popular freedom has grown up with mushroom growth within the last hundred years, and has assumed gigantic dimensions. Corruption of English judges too is a thing of the past; and the argument, that the common sense of a dozen ordinary men may be more depended upon than the refined judgment of an experienced judge, certainly hears well in theory but is hardly found to be sound in practice.

If then jury trials in England be a thing that may be dispensed with, in India the system has proved positively injurious. Those who are familiarly acquainted with the proceedings in our Sessions Courts must be fully aware of the fact that our Juries, consisting mostly of uneducated shopkeepers and petty traders, are often blinded by gross prejudices, and are influenced by a variety of sympathies and antipathies utterly inconsistent with the administration of impartial justice. The reluctance betrayed by jurymen to convict Brahmans, and women, and prisoners well born or connected, is but too well known, and cases not unfrequently happen of the grossest injustice, in which foul offenders are set free because they succeed in winning the sympathy of jurymen. In a word, juries in our country are too often betrayed into a lamentable weakness in favor of the influential as against the lowly,—in favor of the rich as against the poor.

But there is a still greater act of injustice perpetrated by another class of jurymen in this country,—an injustice perpetrated in favor of the White as against the Black. There can be no winking at the fact,—and we hardly think our European readers will deny it either, that a European sinning against an Indian has hardly a fair chance of conviction, in the High Court in Calcutta. It is well known that the men who generally compose the jury in such cases do not by any means represent the educated and enlightened portion of Englishmen in India; and justice and mercy are unhesitatingly sacrificed to national prejudice. The English in this country are jealously guarded from every possible form of injustice that may proceed from national prejudice, and the meanest English loafer is guarded by a halo of sacredness which the Indian magistrate of the highest rank and respectability must not dare to violate.

We do not object to the jealousy with which English prestige is guarded,—indeed such objections would all be made in vain. Let all the cases in which Europeans are the defendants be tried by Europeans, but let it be European Magistrates or Judges and not European juries. We shall willingly confide in the educated and enlightened European for the redress of our grievances even when a European is the offender. But we may not, we cannot, confide in European juries.

The jury system has been weighed in the balance and found wanting. Nowhere in Bengal does it serve the purposes of securing the liberties of the people; for, of all criminal courts, the proceedings of Sessions Courts and the High Court are the least arbitrary, and most widely published. The judges in these courts cannot in any conceivable case be supposed to entertain a grudge against the prisoner, and there is therefore no chance of the liberties of the people being threatened in these courts. And yet in these courts alone we have the jury system prevailing. The system therefore does no good, and the sooner it is done away with the better. But of this enough.

But the most important defect in the present system of administration of justice consists, as we stated at the beginning of this chapter, in the difficulty of ascertaining real facts; and this difficulty is the more singular in a country in which news travels wonderfully fast, and a neighbour is hardly ever ignorant of what his neighbour does. Weakness and dependence on neighbours are among the most marked characteristics of the people of Bengal, and the frequent interchange of services and help is with them a matter of necessity and an every-day and every-hour occurrence. The Bengali considers it a part of his duty to help his neighbours in need, and it is a part of his expectations that his neighbours will help him in need. Naturally enough, the connexion between him and his neighbours is close and intimate, and every one is thoroughly conversant with his neighbour's affairs. Foreigners, who are more exclusive and self-reliant, can hardly have an adequate idea as to how very close this connection is. Almost every villager knows perfectly well every thing that happens to his fellow-villager, and there is hardly a single case coming before our criminal courts about which every particular villager does not know the real facts. But the distance at which our courts are placed from particular villages, coupled with the introduction of a foreign and complicated system of law of evidence, has effectually precluded every possibility of the courts' deriving any benefit from this general knowledge among the villagers. While therefore the facts of any particular case are clearly and widely known and loudly trumpeted throughout the length and breadth of the village, the hard working and conscientious magistrate, carefully debarred from such evidence, perspires from head to foot to make out the truth from a mass of false swearing and exaggerations put forward by so-called eye-witnesses. Surely, in the eye of the simple villager the whole proceeding appears as an ingenious mockery of justice, and he would almost wonder why the Magistrate would not stoop to learn the real facts in the same way in which he himself had learnt them.

But the failure of justice in particular cases is not the worst consequence;—this system of administering justice carries with it a demoralizing effect among the people, which cannot be too strongly censured. People have learnt that the court is determined to act only on the testimony of so-called eye-witnesses produced in the court from a distance sometimes of 20 or 30 miles. To get up such witnesses, to coach them thoroughly as to what they are to say in a court of justice, to give them lessons in lying and false swearing—these are the proper means to win a case; and people are not slow to adopt such means when their efficacy is proved every day and every hour. Fraud and chicanery are increasing, and the present system of administration is thus contaminating the morals of the villagers of Bengal.

But though we have been free in exposing the evil effects proceeding from the difficulty felt by our courts in ascertaining facts, we hardly see any way in which this difficulty may be got over. We are certainly not prepared to recommend the old systems which prevailed in this country, for we cannot forget the *nuzzurs*, the bribery and corruption which such systems fostered. An attempt may however be made with advantage to revive the ancient Panchayets of Bengal. The people of every village might be called upon to nominate a dozen or more persons, say once every year, to serve as members of the village Panchayet, and decide all petty cases *when the parties are willing* to refer their cases to such Panchayets; and the courts might confirm the verdict of such Panchayets unless they see strong reasons to the contrary. Even in important cases the Panchayet might be consulted by the court, or asked to send up a report, and the rigour of English laws of evidence might be relaxed to admit some particular classes of hearsay evidence for the ends of justice. We cannot but think that substantial justice might be much better done by allowing the villagers an important share in its administration. At the same time such an arrangement may be calculated to infuse public spirit and a love of justice among our villagers, and give them practical lessons in the art of administering their own villages, and electing their own representatives.

In the second place, we would strongly recommend the abolition of the mukteari system as it prevails at present in our country. In principle little could be urged against an ignorant ryot being helped and represented in court by a person comparatively speaking versed in law, but those only who have thoroughly examined the actual working of the system are aware of the prodigious evil which it fosters. The muktears coach parties and witnesses in falsehood invented for the occasion, and invest simple cases with huge fabrications, and so attempt to defeat the purposes of justice. Their profession is chicanery, their aim is deceiving, their work is contaminating the morals of a simple agricultural population of the country.

We do not know how far even the employment of Barristers and Vakeels by private parties in the superior courts serves the purposes of justice. The rich criminal secures the highest talent and eloquence to screen him from deserved punishment, the poor man who seeks justice has none to advocate his claims and many to oppose them. We confess we have grave doubts as to whether these circumstances are conducive to the interests of justice, or whether the conscious exerting of talents in the cause of falsehood is honorable to a profession. And yet the difference between Barristers and Muktears is very great indeed. Barristers and Vakeels, generally speaking, try to represent their cases in the best light,—muktears distort facts, coach up witnesses, deal in lies. Besides, in the higher courts where the procedure is somewhat complicated, some persons versed in law and the rules of the court are probably necessary to avoid the confusion which would otherwise almost inevitably arise from the ignorance of the clients. In the mofussil criminal courts, on the other hand, the procedure is exceedingly simple, and except perhaps in a few serious cases the clients need not be represented at all. To conduct these serious cases,—or if it is thought desirable,—to conduct all cases, two Government pleaders might be appointed to each court (for prosecution and defence) who, while fairly representing their clients' cases to the court, would not have the motive for falsehood which characterize the muktears. The ryots, released from the grasp of the muktears, will cheerfully pay an additional fee which will more than indemnify Government for the extra cost of keeping two vakeels for each court;—and the arrangement is certain to produce a degree of good to the country which it is scarcely possible to conceive. In our humble opinion, this plan may with advantage be extended to the higher courts.

Next come in the Amlahs of our courts, humble to servility before the Hákim, haughty and overbearing towards all outsiders, and in corruptness and dishonesty yielding to no class of people on the face of the earth. Surrounded by coached up and therefore perjured witnesses, lying and misleading Muktears, a corrupt police, and Amlahs deeply bribed,—bound down by law to a system of procedure the least adapted to the eliciting of truth,—compelled to rely on the so-called evidence rather than to his own shrewdness and the probabilities of the case,—what wonder if the most intelligent Magistrate will sometimes totally fail to arrive at the truth?

To remedy this, our Magistrates themselves should have more opportunities of ascertaining the facts of cases, and this can only be done by increasing their number, and placing a Magistrate almost in every Thana, so that he may see with his own eyes almost every thing that passes in the Mofussil. Called upon to administer only about 50 or 60 villages of a Thana, all within the radius of 5 or 6 miles from his court, such a Magistrate may well be expected to have a thorough acquaintance with every one of such villages. At present the police officer in charge of the Thana has such experience, but shameless corruption pervades and pollutes the ranks of the police, and the present Magistrates cannot place any reliance on the more complete and far-reaching knowledge of the police officers. What is wanted, therefore, is the complete merging of the police in the judicial,—the eliminating of big police appointments, and increasing the number of judicial authorities. But this brings us to the important subject of the police, and we must here pause and make a few remarks on this subject.

Time was when the police of Bengal was the dread of the land, when a dacoity was doubly dreaded because a police investigation was to follow ; and up to the present day the traditions of Bengal are replete with police-oppression remembrances. Act V. of 1861 was passed to remedy this state of things, and it is worth while enquiring how far matters have improved since then. Physical torture used to be applied in olden times for the purpose of extorting confession from prisoners or coaching up witnesses. Physical torture is applied in the present day too, but much less frequently, and the torture inflicted in the present day is mild and humane compared with the cruelties of the old police which often ended in death. The corruption of the police too has decreased in respect of the amount of bribes received, but in other respects is as widespread as ever. The corruption of the police is often complained of, but few are aware of the extent to which it prevails in this country. Few have realized to themselves the astounding fact that not one per cent of constables and head constables are above corruption, and that even among Inspectors and Sub-Inspectors an honest man is an exception. The few improvements mentioned above have been caused not by the Act V. of 1861, but by the creation of Sub-divisions which, by bringing the Magistrates near the scene of action as it were, has been productive of greater good to the country in a variety of ways than almost any other administrative measure that may be named. Thirteen years have elapsed since the passing of the Police Act, every attempt has been made to raise the stamina of the police,—the pay of an Inspector of police has been increased to Rs. 250, *i. e.* the pay of a Munsiff, and certainly a respectable pay for a post of that nature; a fair trial, therefore, it may be supposed, has been given to this Act, and after such trial the Act has failed most ignominiously.

Nor are the reasons of such failure far to seek. The honesty of a particular man may depend on a variety of circumstances, but the honesty of a class of men, it may be taken for granted as a maxim, will always vary in inverse ratio to the temptations offered. A service therefore which holds out ample temptations for dishonesty, and very faint threats of detection and punishment, may be presumed *a priori* to be tainted with corruption, and police service is precisely and pre-eminently such a one. The only measure therefore likely to prove effective would be, somehow to increase the chances of detection, until every act of dishonesty committed in town or in village by the police has at least a fair chance of being detected and visited with punishment.

But how is this to be effected? We have already hinted at the answer before. Under recent orders and circulars the District Superintendents of police have been made almost completely subordinate to the Magistrates;—why then retain that highly paid post? A large saving may be effected by abolishing the post of District Superintendents, and distributing their work among the Inspectors and the Magistrate's subordinates and clerks. A large saving too may be effected by keeping a Sub-Inspector in every Sub-division (instead of an Inspector,) making him completety subordinate to the sub-divisional officer. Such saving might be very beneficially spent in placing small paid sub-magistrates in charge of Thanas, who would be subordinate to the subdivisional officers in the same way in which subdivisional officers are subordinate to district officers. Of police, a Head Constable would be quite enough for a Thana,—such Head Constable being made completely subordinate to the Thana judicial officer. Such multiplying of judicial officers, and merging of the police in the judicial may be calculated to be of the greatest possible good to the country. By such an arrangement courts will be brought almost to the door of every sufferer who may seek for justice, and Magistrates too will be able to see almost with their own eyes whatever passes in the Mofussil. Such a system too cannot but impart solace and assurance to the much-oppressed ryot of Bengal, for he cannot but be inspired with confidence by seeing within a few miles of his own home a power capable of curbing the much-dreaded Naeb and Gomashta.

Lastly, we would advocate a thorough reform in the village chowkedari system. It is a complaint all over the country that chowkedars are negligent of their duties, and in most cases are themselves the abettors of theft and receivers of stolen property. The reason lies in a nutshell;—chowkedars do not receive their pay! While chowkedars are responsible to police authorities for any negligence,—by a strange oversight in legislation no provision is made for their pay,—except in the very few places where the Chowkedari Act is in force. To be sure villagers are directed to pay so much each to the chowkedar as his pay, but if the payment is refused there is no provision of law to compel the same. It happens therefore that in most places chowkedars are very scantily paid by the villagers, and in places where the chowkedars may have disgusted some influential villagers by tracing out some serious cases of theft,—he may be sure of not receiving a pice from the villagers for years to come. The chowkedars are therefore naturally enough negligent of their duties, and anxious to eke out their small pay by other employments, and thus one of the earliest and most useful institutions of the countries, the village watch system, is, by a sad mistake in legislation, getting day by day hopelessly deranged. And yet it is not too late yet,—nor is the remedy far to seek. Nothing is simpler than to enable magistrates to levy on all villagers the pay of the chowkedars, and then to bring the chowkedars themselves under a vigorous control, and to a lively sense of their duties.

We have dwelt so long on the subject of the administration of criminal justice that we must content ourselves with a few passing observations on our civil courts, and we shall confine our remarks to the two important and crying grievances, *viz.*, inordinate expenditure and delay consequent to civil proceedings. The number of our civil courts has been increased since the English came to this country, but a still larger increase is, we believe, necessary in consequence of the entire change which has taken place in the system of the collection of revenue. The demands of the Mahommedan rulers on the land-owners and zemindars were peremptory and exceedingly arbitrary, and varied with the wants and exigencies of the state, and the peaceful or troublesome nature of the times; but these rulers, consistent in their oppressive principle, also allowed such zemindars the exercise of powers equally arbitrary and oppressive on their dependent tenants and ryots. It followed that the ryots could hardly as a matter of right object to the demands of their zemindars, any more than the zemindars could object to the demands of the Subadar's underlings. In the absence of all right therefore, the only effectual checks on the demands of the masters, and the only thing which the rent-payers could urge with any chance of getting a hearing were, firstly, the chance of the ruin of the rent-payers which would stop up the source of revenue, and, secondly, the immemorial custom of the land which among all patriarchal nations answers the purposes of right, and stretches a helping hand to the poor, being often recognized as inviolate even by arbitrary despots. Under such circumstances, civil courts were not necessary in revenue matters,—indeed the realization of revenue was considered so important that even criminal courts would hardly interfere to save the wretched ryot from beating and confinement who had failed to pay his rent. The English in India have ushered in a mighty change. They have imported into India the all-important notion of *right* as it is understood in Western Europe, and they decline to recognize the inviolability even of custom, unless the custom is embalmed and perpetuated by being converted into a right. The English rule has declared, and rightly declared, that the ryot, the tenant and the zemindar, will all have their rights and duties created by laws, and even the imperial Government will be subjected to laws of its own creation and invested with rights and duties. A net work of civil courts therefore is necessary in order to the enforcing of such rights; and while, under the old regime, a custom might be enforced by one's taking up the law in his own hand; under the new regime, courts must be applied to in order to enforcing of a right,—and indeed in every step in the process of collecting and realizing rent. Thus the salutary change in the system of collecting rents requires a vast increase in the number of civil courts.

Have the courts been increased proportionately to the requirements? Painful experience proves the contrary. Poor people quarrelling among themselves about bits of land are loathe to incur the expense and the trouble of dancing attendance on civil courts which are too few in number to do all their work with speed, and often seek redress in criminal courts by disguising their civil dispute in a criminal form, and seek such redress in vain. Zemindars complain with justice, but complain in vain, that the British Government, while rigorously strict in exacting rent in stated times, affords them no means of exacting rent with equal regularity from their dependent tenants and ryots. The ryots complain with justice, but complain in vain, that the kind care manifested by the British Government in the Revenue Laws to protect their interest is all in vain, for the remedy afforded therein, *viz.*, by complaining in civil courts against unjust exactions and unlawful ousting, is too expensive for them to adopt; and law therefore is in many cases a dead letter to them. All the painful consequences which attend the withholding of justice are observed to ensue, in a mitigated form though it be, from the fact of our civil courts chasing off litigants by the dreary prospect of expense and delay which they hold out. The Naebs and Gomashtas turn their faces against such courts, and exact rent from obstinate ryots in the primitive way, *viz.*, by beating and wrongful confinement; and the ryots themselves often take the law in their own hands, and decide with clubs and sticks their disputes, which our civil courts decline to decide within a reasonable time and expense. It is admitted on all hands that the relation between zemindars and ryots is daily becoming more unsatisfactory. We may certainly blame the ryot to a certain extent for their conduct, or we may blame the zemindar; but the root of this evil is undoubtedly to be sought for in the revenue laws of the country and the system of revenue administration. Indeed, nothing reflects so unfavourably on the British system of revenue administration in India as the fact that, among a race of peasantry so peaceful as that of Bengal, feuds and rioting and landed disputes are a daily occurrence. The Bengali is naturally so averse to actual violence and warfare that, so long as there is the remotest possibility of justice being obtained at a court of *law*, he will not go to actual fighting; and it is only when our civil courts literally scare him away with a cheerless prospect of delay and expense that he involuntarily has recourse to the last means left.

To take an instance; a zemindar wants to increase the rent payable by the occupier of a certain bit of land. The course prescribed by law is a reference to the civil court whose decision would be final and definite. But the zemindar knows but too well the cost of such a reference, and therefore has recourse to what he believes to be an easier and simpler method. If he is strong enough, he uses compulsion,—if not, he takes to ingenious tricks. He grants a pottah to a new ryot who consents to pay the increased rent for the bit of land in question, and thus a dispute ensues between the new man and the old man with reference to the identical bit of land. The old ryot may complain in a civil court against this intrusion into his ancient possession,—or the new ryot may complain against any opposition to his right based on a registered pottah,—but both involuntarily turn from the very name of a civil court; and carry on their disputes as best they may, sometimes for years together. Indeed, under the present system of administration, it is sometimes the interest of the zemindar to try to oust an occupancy ryot by such underhand practices. Supposing the chance a zemindar has in succeeding in such unjust claims is one to four,—it surely is a profitable investment with him to pay costs of three or four suits in order to permanently though unjustly increase the rent of a piece of land. Hence it is that we find in the Mofussil innumerable instances of feuds and rioting between two parties,—one the ancient occupier of a bit of land, the other a new man backed with a newly registered pottah granted by the zemindar. In the civil court their case like a wounded snake drags its slow length along,—but in the meantime at every sowing and reaping season some rioting is sure to take place with respect to the disputed land,—and the criminal court is compelled to chastise both parties once in six months,—while the zemindar quietly sits in his Kachari, watching the game with interest and laughing in his sleeves. In a second instance, a ryot is justly or unjustly ousted. A reference to a civil court would no doubt right matters,

—but it would so perhaps after a year,—and his ruin would by that time be complete. He naturally, if not justly, sticks to his old soil and homestead, prepared to defend his rights against any new comer who may present himself, and if the worst comes to the worst, then and not till then to refer to the civil court. In a third instance, entire villages become annoyed with their master, and in a fit of indiscretion declare that their zemindar shall levy no rent. What is the poor zemindar to do? The law prescribes a reference to the civil court for levying rent on every particular ryot who refuses to pay his due. The law forgets that long before a zemindar can levy rent in this way,—a work of years,—his estates and lands would all be sold for arrears of revenue payable to Government. It is easy to multiply instances,—but *qui bono?*

It is necessary vividly to realize the fact that the delay and expenditure incident to rent cases are productive of incalculable harm both to the zemindar and to the ryot. It is necessary to understand clearly that ninety per cent. of the cases of rioting and landed feuds, that go up to our criminal courts, would never have occurred but for the fact, that our revenue courts cannot decide cases within a reasonable time and at a reasonable cost. And it is necessary to keep in mind the fact that, among a people so thoroughly agricultural as that of Bengal,—and especially where almost every individual ryot has his set of rights to hold up,—those courts, which are the only means to declare and maintain such rights, should be especially quick and not especially tardy in their operations. There are reasons historical if not sensible why civil law in England was, up to a very late period, and to a certain extent is, even now, hampered and encrusted over with a mass of almost unintelligible forms and rules. The busy schoolmen of the middle ages assiduously handed down to modern nations precepts and legal forms of the old Roman law, and such forms were embalmed by their very antiquity. The English among other modern nations found themselves in the 15th and 16th centuries of the Christian era almost unconsciously led to the ancient notions and forms. For good or for evil, the judges of England for centuries together borrowed vastly from the ancient law under the disguise of simply administering the law of the land. Thus grew up gradually the precepts and rules, the presumptions and forms of English law,—a mighty and heterogeneous mass, but certainly a singular study for the historian and the antiquarian. For centuries together that mighty fabric defied the hand of revolution or legislation. The vitality of English institutions is well known, but nowhere does it more conspicuously manifest itself than in the subject of law. Every crude form, every obsolete precept, every practice which at any time prevailed in Westminster, seemed to be especially guarded from rational change by the traditions of the bar and the dignity of the bench.

But such forms and precepts and practices when imported to India lose their historical harmony and antiquarian value, and prove a pure nuisance. We see no reason therefore why traces of such practices, which remain after the passing of the Act VIII. of 1859, should not at once be removed. At the same time the procedure of civil courts still admits of further simplification.

Lastly, Munsiffs themselves should be strongly impressed with a lively sense of their duty in doing things with despatch. In spite of the legal drawbacks mentioned before, rent cases were decided speedily enough by executive officers before the Act VIII. of 1869 was passed;—and now that the duty has passed into the hands of the civil courts we do not see why these courts should not be called upon to use the same despatch in their work. We do not by any means intend to cast any reflection on civil officers generally,—on the contrary, we are aware of the fact that the work which many of them have to do is a giant's work, and we have ourselves advocated elsewhere the multiplying of civil courts. But at the same time we cannot wink at the fact, that the want of a proper supervision makes *some* civil officers extremely tardy in their work. Something of the spirit of despatch which characterizes the executive service should be infused into the judicial,—and this can only be done by the superior authorities impressing the fact on the civil courts that, next to deciding cases with impartiality and justice, their most important duty is to decide cases with *des-*

patch; and further that this last subject will invariably be taken into consideration in weighing the relative claims of civil officers to promotion. Unless the courts are made more alive to this part of their duty all changes in law and procedure will be useless.

Under this head we need only mention that, throughout the country, it is a matter of regret with the peasantry that rent cases are now decided by civil courts instead of by executive officers,—and the cause of the regret is simply the increased delay incident to the new mode of procedure. We do not advocate the bringing about the old state of things, but some wholesale improvement in the procedure of our revenue courts is urgently required.

We have confined our remarks almost entirely to revenue cases, because Bengal is so thoroughly an agricultural country that a very large proportion of cases that come before our civil courts are rent-suits. But our remarks apply equally well to pure civil cases, and people of all denominations will hail the day when the gates of justice will be opened wide to the rich and poor alike.

We shall here conclude. We have strongly recommended the multiplying of cases, both civil and criminal, and our reasons lie in a nut-shell. The oriental mind has always associated power with oppression,—power with the abuse of power. The annals of centuries have only strengthened the association and turned it into a fixed idea. To disabuse the mind of such a servile association is a gigantic task, but the attempt should be made. The attempt has been made, and with success too, among the *educated* people of this country; but when will the attempt succeed with the *masses?* The popular mind is still as staunch a believer of oppression being one of the attributes of power, as stern a disbeliever in right independently of might, as it ever was; and the head-and-tail system of justice as administered in our courts not unoften appears to them as a concession in favor of tact and money as against poverty and stupidity. Is it worth while to shew to the popular mind instances of power unattended with oppression, of right existing independently of might? Is it worth while to impress on the popular mind,—even as it has already been thoroughly impressed on the educated mind in Bengal,—ideas of right and justice as they are understood in Western Europe? Then the only way is to multiply our courts, and to afford the poor man means of obtaining justice almost at his own door. The notion of right is a noble one, but we hope it will not be said of it hereafter in this country, that it was a noble idea that died with John Bull.

CHAPTER VI.

VILLAGE INDUSTRY.

> Let not ambition mock their useful toil,
> Their homely joys and destiny obscure,
> Nor grandeur hear with a disdainful smile
> The short and simple annals of the poor.
>
> GRAY.

To travel among rice plains and jungly vegetation, among groups of lowly huts, clumps of bamboos and mangoe topes covering and darkening the villages, with no other companions than the simple and wretched villagers, now sowing the *Aûsh dhan* under the midday sun, and now dragged to the zemindar's *kachari* for inability to pay rent,—how many of you, neatly dressed Babus of Calcutta, will accompany us in this rustic undertaking? How many of you will care to accompany us through dark, jungly, perhaps malarious villages that may give you the fever,—how many of you will travel through almost unending fields of corn under the midday sun which may give you the sun-stroke? Few we apprehend. But if there are any who consider the task of investigating into the habits and occupations of considerably over half of the people of Bengal as an interesting one,—who amid the astounding progress of our towns have cast a sorrowful look towards the stagnant condition of their brethren of the villages,—who have in solitary moments thought and felt within themselves that the true progress of this country will only commence when the poor Bengal ryot will be bettered in condition,—such we shall gladly have as our companions in our sojourn in the villages, and to such we commend this chapter.

The Bengali year commences with the month of Baisakh (April, May,) and agricultural work in Bengal may also be said to commence with that month. Fields parched up by the rainless winter and spring of Bengal are ploughed up by the cultivators early in Baisakh, and the first rains of this month are hailed as a warning that the time for *Aush* sowings has come. After a long dry season the earth receives as with grateful joy the first showers of Baisakh, and the cultivators with no less joy and gratitude begin their *Aûsh* sowings on the moistened face of the earth.

It is well known that the two great classes of rice in Bengal are the *Aush* and the *Aman*. The *Aush* is sown early as we have seen and grows on high lands, and is reaped early too, *viz.* in the month of Bhadra (August, September.) The name is probably derived from the word *asu* which means early. The *Aman* on the other hand almost feeds entirely on rain, and is sown on low lands which are inundated year after year. The name is a corruption of the word *Haimanta* which means autumnal, as it is in autumn that fields of *Aman* are seen stretching on every side like a sea of waving green. It is sown rather late, *viz.*, in Ashadh (June, July) when heavy rains have moistened and almost inundated the earth, and reaped late in the Bengali year, *viz.* in Agraháyana and Pous (December.) The *Aman* is the finer and dearer sort of rice used by the middle and upper classes of Bengal, and is of various kinds such as *Dádkháni*, *Bálám*, &c. The *Aûsh* is cheaper and coarser, and used only by poor people and the villagers.

In the annual rice sowings the Mahájan has an important part to play, and we must therefore make a few observations relating to him. The mahájans discharge a very important function in the social economy of Bengal, so important indeed, that all agricultural work would be at a stand-still without their assistance. The improvidence of the Bengal ryot is well known,—indeed it is the natural result of the circumstances under which he is placed and has been placed for centuries together. What with the exactions of subadars and zemindars and taxgatherers, what with the ravages of external and internal war, and what with the periodical devastation of predatory races, security was never known to the poor people of India. Even to the present day the relationship existing between the zemindars and the ryots do not, we are bound to say, foster habits of foresight and prudence among the people. All these circumstances have had their influence on the formation of the character of the Indian peasant and made him what he is—a creature without foresight, caring only for to-day and unable or unwilling to provide for to-morrow. When therefore that to-morrow comes,—when the ryot wants money either to pay a tax or for his own support,—either to pay the zemindar's rent or to sow his lands, he must borrow money or *dhan* at any rate at which it can be had; and exorbitant rates have naturally raised a class of people who following different pursuits of life depend mainly on lending money. Nor is it the ryot alone who is so improvident. The Zemindar, the Taluqdar, the Gantidar, every one resorts to the Maháján in times of need, and resorts to him not in vain. People who know little of village life have been startled at hearing the rates of interest (which are never less than 25 per cent, and seldom less than 37½ per cent) at which mahájans lend their money and *dhan*; and proposals are often made to put a stop to this sort of thing by Government interference. We are afraid such steps if taken will produce much harm and no good. The prudence and foresight of the money-lenders compensate for the improvidence of the entire village population of Bengal; and they, as a body, save entire classes of people from utter ruin year after year. Many of the zemindars could pay revenue to Government every year independently of the assistance of the mahájans, and hardly 10 per cent. of the ryots could without such assistance carry on their agricultural work year after year. They borrow *dhan* mostly in Baisákh for the purposes of sowing as well as to live upon, and pay off this agricultural debt at a high rate of interest either at the *Aúsh* harvest in Bhadra, or at the *Aman* harvest in Magh. Nor would the rates seem exorbitant when we consider it a tax which shameless improvidence pays to the only means that can save it from ruin,—when we further consider the risk undertaken, the difficulties which often attend recovery, and above all the universality of the demand. Indeed in this case, as in every other case of a similar nature, the laws of demand and supply regulate and determine the rates, and government interference will only create mischief. Any usury laws that may be enacted are sure to be evaded, and the poor ryots,—the borrowers,—would have to pay the cost of such illegal evasion over and above the rates.

We hope we shall not be mistaken. It is not our intention to defend money-lending as a profession;—we admit all that has been said against it, we admit it has a demoralizing effect on those who borrow, and smothers all noble feelings in those who lend, by teaching them to extort their heartless gain in the coolest and cruellest manner from starving poverty and distress. But admitting all this, we maintain that the profession has become a necessity and settled down into a custom, and Government interference will only do harm. Is it expected that a single enactment will in one day change the improvident habits which the people, as we have already seen, have acquired in centuries? If not, the only other means to do away with money lending at high rates would be for Government to advance money and *dhan* at smaller rates,—taking upon themselves the burdensome duty of realizing their loans from poor ryots. We hardly believe our Government are prepared to go so far, as it would involve them in endless complications and law-suits. Then, there is simply *no* other alternative than to leave matters alone. But to return to our story from our long digression.

We have seen fields ploughed up and *Aûsh* sown early in Baisákh (April, May); Baisákh and Jyastha pass on, raïns increase, until in Ashadh (June, July) the skies assume a darksome aspect and rain comes down in torrents. The rainy season in Bengal is certainly one of the most magnificent phenomena that nature presents in any part of the world, though it fails to strike us on account of our familiarity with it. Skies are filled with deep purple clouds darkening the atmosphere with an aspect of terror and unearthly gloom, lurid flashes of lightning dazzle the eye with their uncommon brilliancy, loud booms of thunder reverberating through the wide atmosphere proclaim to an awe-struck world the wrath of Heaven, storms and cyclones of excessive might batter down huts and trees and howl and sweep across the devoted country with the fury of infernal beings, and torrents of rain such as may be witnessed in very few countries deluge fields and meadows and make rivers inundate entire districts. Miles and miles together in districts near the Sunderbunds remain under water knee-deep or waist-deep for months, and villages which are built on elevated tracts of lands appear like floating islands surrounded by wide masses of waters. It is in such districts that *Aman* grows in superabundance. The Ganges becomes extraordinarily powerful during the rainy weather, spreading her sea-like expanse over miles and miles together, and sweeping away thousands of acres and entire villages in her imperious wrath.

During this inclement weather the peasant does not remain idle. Nursed by the heavy rains the *Aûsh* shoots up rapidly, but with *Aush* also shoot up grass and weeds to choke its growth, and it is only by repeated weeding that the corn retains its health. Nor is weeding by any means a pleasant affair. Toiling in mud and mire, insensible of wind and rain, the peasant looks after his corn with the affection of a parent and is never tired of doing any thing and every thing conducive to a good harvest. Nor must we here forget to mention that it is in this season that *Aman* is sown. It is in the month of Ashadh when lands are well saturated with rain that *Aman* is sown on low lands, and with increasing rain the *dhan* shoots up with mushroom growth.* But of this hereafter.

---

* Some species of *Aman* are however sown along with *Aûsh* in Baisakh. They grow together on the same soil, and when *Aûsh* is reaped in Bhadra, *Aman* is allowed to remain standing and is reaped along with other species of *Aman* in Pous. Properly speaking these species only, thus sown early with *Aush* are called *Aman* while the dhan that is sown in Asadh and transplanted in Sraban and Bhadra, is called *roa* which is a corruption of the Sanskrit *ropita* or transplanted.

Ashadh passes on, and by the latter end of Sraban (July, August) the *Aush* gets ripe, and the harvest fairly sets in in Bhādra (August, September.) Rural prospects in Bhadra are by no means uninteresting. Trees and shrubs and thick groves, washed by recent showers and sparkling under the Indian sun, present a peculiarly fresh and cheerful aspect, and interminable fields of waving golden corn spread their vast sea-like expanse on every side of the rural wayfarer. And now the *Aush* harvest begins. The ryots view with joy the fields of uniform gold that stretch before their eye and begin their pleasant work at once.

Aush is reaped and gathered.—Where?—In the barn houses of the ryots?—Alas! no. The mahajans who lent their money and dhan must now be paid at a high rate of interest. If money was lent, the rate of interest is generally 37½ per cent, and if *dhan* was lent in Baisakh,—half as much again (*derhi*) must be paid back by the end of Bhadra. Then again the Zemindar, whose claims, legal as well as illegal, the royt can hardly ever pay off in full, comes upon the poor ryot at this harvest time, and when their dues are paid or partly paid, the ryot,—he who has laboured in morning and in evening, in mud and in mire, in rain, wind and hail, for growing the crops,—has little left to carry home. Alas poor Bengal ryot! when will education enable thee to hold thy own against all others and make thee a prudent, provident and independent creature?

Harvest is a pleasant thing all over the world, and certainly it is not the least pleasant in Bengal. In Italy, France, and other vine-producing countries the festivities at vintage gladden the villagers after their annual labor, and certainly the Hindus whose joyousness of spirit is peculiarly adapted to festivities and celebrations yield neither to the Italian nor to the French. The season too is the pleasantest in the year. The heat of summer has departed, and yet winter has not yet come in, rains have disappeared, waters have subsided or are fast subsiding, and the earth rising as it were from a salubrious bath appears in fresher loveliness and richer green. In such a delightful season the *Aush* harvest closes with Bhadra, and Aswin (September, October) therefore witnesses the commencement of a series of festivities equalled in no other part of the world. A beautiful custom draws together brother and sister on the last day of the Durga Puja,—draws together parent and children, husband and wife, master and servant, friend and friend,—aye the most distant relatives, to embrace and bless each other with fulness of heart.

We have viewed the Puja as a harvest festival. It must be admitted, however, that at present it has very little of the character of a harvest festival, though it undoubtedly originated as such. Nor is it difficult to conjecture the causes which have led to this change. Bengal has always been pre-eminently an agricultural country, and with the exception of Government officers, almost the entire population, including shopkeepers and money-lenders, traders and merchants, were intimately connected with villages and village-life, and often had acres of land of their own ;—and indeed had their *homes* in villages though most of them lived in towns for the greater part of the year to conduct business. A large portion of the money therefore that accumulated in the country was often spent in villages on various occasions, and on all these occasions the ryots were allowed freely to mingle and share in the joy and festivities. Thus, though the ryots had never probably the competence to indulge in the luxury of Pujas and celebrations themselves, the fact of their freely mingling in the festivities, held by the *matabbar* men in the village immediately after the harvest, gave such celebrations pre-eminently the character of harvest festivals. Two causes have operated in the way of putting a stop to this state of things. The Mahommedan rulers of our country vigorously proselytized the people, till, as we now find, almost half the agriculturists and cultivators changed their religion, and with their religion gave up their ancient usages. A second and, perhaps, a still more potent cause will be found in the fact of the contact of this country with European civilization. Among the many latent but important results of which this contact has been the cause,—not the least important result will be found in the increased importance with which towns are invested, and the wide gulf which has been created between towns and villages. European notions of utility and division of labor have caused a general rush of all well-to-do people towards towns, and a desertion of villages to the cultivators. Few will be inclined to question that this is a fact. Nine-tenths of the well-to-do people who have now settled down in Calcutta and the suburbs will be able to trace, that their ancestors at no distant date were villagers, or at least had their *homes* in villages though they may have frequented towns often enough. Thus towns are in the present day daily increasing in magnitude and importance, and the wealth of the country is spent in towns. Pujas too have migrated from villages to towns along with those who are competent to celebrate them, and have almost grown into a town institution,—though even now zemindars and other well-to-do people celebrate them in the moffussil. But to our story.

We have seen *Aman* (the species called *roa*) sown in nurseries, or small plots of lands near the cultivator's house, in the month of Ashadh. There is a main distinction between the *Aman* and the *Aush* as regards the seasons favorable to their growth. *Aman* suffers in drought, and *Aush* in years of excessive rain, and it is only in years of moderate rain-fall that both crops flourish. *Aman* requires no weeding, it increases with increasing rain, but when little plants have shot up they must be transplanted. The process of transplantation is rather an arduous one, as the plants which have grown promiscuously in nurseries have to be taken one by one and arranged in uniform rows in the fields so that they may grow healthily and steadily. Much rain is wanted in the season of transplanting, but when once transplanted, the *Aman* requires no more looking after. Transplantation generally takes place in Bhadra (August, September.)

Aswin (September, October,) and Kartik (October, November,) are comparatively speaking months of idleness among the peasantry, in so far at least as the rice harvests are concerned, and the Puja festivities which commence in Aswin are continued almost unremittingly throughout Kartik. By the middle of Aughran (November, December,) the *Aman* is ripe and harvest fairly sets in at the latter end of that month.

We shall not here forget to mention the temporary emigration which takes place in Pous, (December, January) year after year in Bengal. We have stated before that *Aman* grows best in inundated tracts; and the districts bordering on the Sunderbunds, which are inundated year after year, produce a plentiful supply of *Aman* more than the cultivators can hope to reap unaided. And as this *Aman* ripens somewhat later than *Aman* in other parts of the country, laborers from all parts can afford, after reaping the *Aman* of their own villages, to swarm to the Sunderbunds in large numbers with the certain hope of finding work in the *Aman*-reaping time; and in this hope they are never disappointed. Thus peasants from all parts of the country crowd to these districts unmindful of malarious atmosphere, of risk, danger and death, each peasant presenting himself to the master under whom he worked in the preceding year, and returning to his own village after corn is reaped, with his fixed quantum of corn as his wages. This annual trip of thousands and tens of thousands of people to the Sunderbunds forms, it must be confessed, a curious commentary on the proceedings of the planters of Bengal. The employers of labor in the Sunderbunds have no agents, they promise no exorbitant wages, they do not provide against risk or illness, they have no dispensaries even though the field of labor is unhealthy and malarious, they do not even provide for proper accommodation for laborers; and yet laborers crowd to the Sunderbunds with alacrity in spite of astounding drawbacks. Why is it that English planters in Bengal with all their brilliant promises often fail to obtain *willing* laborers? Let each answer the question for himself.

The *Aman* harvest closes with Pous (December, January.) The *Aush* harvest, we have seen, is the cause of much rejoicing. The time of the *Aman* harvest is not so favorable to outdoor merriment, as the cold of Pous keeps people within doors. And yet the people of Bengal recognize the joyousness of the occasion and observe an *in-door* practice which certainly does not yield to the merry Christmas of England in hilarity and merry-making. On the last day of Pous is held the Pous Parban or *Amani* Parban, as it is sometimes called, which means the festival of the *Aman* harvest. Families gather together in joy and observe a variety of little rites and ceremonies, but the chief part of the festival consists, even like the Christmas of cold December, in a warm and hearty dinner, in the preparation and distribution of warm and delicious cakes prepared from a variety of materials.

Thus ends Pous. In Magh (January and February) there is little paddy business. In Falgun (February, March) and Chaitra (March, April) many of the ryots who do not grow any other crops on their lands but rice, plough up their land for rice sowings in Baisakh. With Chaitra closes the Bengali year.

We have dwelt so long on rice, because the cultivation of rice may be said to be the one occupation of our cultivators. In remote villages rice or rather *dhan* serves the purposes of current money. Peasants borrow *dhan* of their Mahajan in small quantities throughout the six months from April to September. With portions of this *dhan* they go to the village shop and get salt or mustard oil in exchange, and sometimes clothing or utensils too are bought not by money but by *dhan*. At the great harvest of September the rural debt is paid off; a few months elapse, and then the same debt is contracted again.

In the remaining portion of this chapter we shall briefly touch upon some other products grown all over Bengal, as also on a few manufactures and articles of trade. We have nothing to do with such things as are produced in towns, and even of village manufactures we intend to give nothing like a detailed description or exhaustive category. We shall merely make brief mention of a few important articles, simply to shew the nature of the work in which our villagers are engaged.

Winter crops are generally grown on *Aush* lands after the dhan is reaped in September, and are reaped in January and February. While therefore the *Aman* lands produce only one crop, the Aush lands generally speaking produce two crops *i. e.*, the dhan and the sort of winter crops sown. On the other hand, good *Aman* lands produce grain year after year while most *Aush* lands have to be left fallow for a year or two after producing crops for three, four, five or more years, according to the fertility of the soil. A variety of crops are thus sown in September* on *Aush* lands after the dhan is harvested, and go by the name of winter crops. Mustard seed, linseed, gram, *arhar*, *teel*, various kinds of *dál*, wheat, barley, &c. are the most important. The prospect of the country about the end of December is by no means uninteresting. Fields of mustard flower appearing like a sheet of dazzling yellow present a pleasing contrast to the rich green linseed plants dotted with beautiful blue flowers, while here and there arhar plants, rising several

* Sometimes they are sown not on *Aush* lands, bnt on lands specially kept and tilled for such crops.

cubits high overshade acres of ground together and afford shelter and shade to the village wayfarer. Wheat and barley are produced in this country in very small quantities. *Arhar* and various kinds of *dál* that are produced are mostly consumed in the villages and towns of Bengal, and the gram produced here is of a very inferior sort and sells at a much cheaper price than the Patna gram. *Teel*, mustard seed and linseed, are used in making oils, and are also largely exported to Europe. After the plants are cut they are taken home by the cultivators and stacked. When the stalks and the pods are dried they are scattered on the ground, and trampled upon by cows, five or six in number, which are tethered to a bamboo pole fixed in the centre. The stocks are then thrown away, and the seed is collected and carefully winnowed. Linseed specially is exported in large quantities to Europe. It is a very important article of commerce and the oil produced from linseed is largely used for painting. Linseed is often mixed with mustard seed to adulterate the mustard oil.

Chillies are also considered as one of the important winter crops, and are largely consumed by villagers. Peas, beans and a variety of vegetables are also grown in winter.

Jute.—Like *Aush* dhan jute is sown after the first fall of rain in Baisakh, the seeds being sown broadcast and covered with a thin layer of earth by a ladder. Jute grows on partially sandy soil ;—the land being dry and above the flood mark. Young plants shoot up, and if the seedlings are found to grow too thick they are thinned by means of a hoe repeatedly drawn over the land. Like *Aush* dhan jute plants become fit for cutting by the end of August or the beginning of September. After the plants are cut they are tied up in small bundles and thrown into stagnant water to rot. After they have so remained for about a fortnight and have become quite rotten, they are taken up, the stocks are broken and the fibre comes out. They are then washed clean and dried in the sun.

The cultivation of jute has considerably increased within the last few years, and in several districts specially in the east, the peasantry have much improved in their condition by jute cultivation. There is considerable diversity of opinions as to whether the production of jute improves or impairs the productive powers of the soil. Another contested point with regard to jute production is whether it is unhealthy. It is generally supposed that the production is not unhealthy, but that the process of rottening the stalks is injurious to health if it takes place in or near villages.

Jute is largely exported to Europe, and the export trade is increasing year after year. It is a very important article of commerce, and is extensively used in the making of stuffs of various kinds, which again return to India from Europe for sale.

Tobacco, like the winter crops, is sown in September and reaped in January, but unlike the winter crops it is never produced on *Aush* fields. On the contrary, separate fields have to be reserved for tobacco cultivation, and tbe greatest pains are bestowed to prepare the tobacco lands. From the beginning of the Bengali year (April) up to September when tobacco is sown, the tobacco lands are ploughed repeatedly and not a single blade of grass is allowed to grow thereon. In September the tobacoo seed is sown in a nursery, aud when small plants have shot up they are (like Aman dhan) transplanted to the carefully prepared and manured lands. The plants are there transplanted in parallel rows, about a cubit or more apart from each other. Tobacco is always grown on high and dry lands, and an admixture of sand is almost invariably preferred. After the young seedlings are thus transplanted some water is required, and if rains cease early such water is got from distant beels and rivers by a rude systom of irrigation canals, which the peasants dig with great perseverance. By the middle of October rains cease, and the broad green leaves look fresh and healthy. By the month of January tobacco becomes fit for cutting, and a single shower of rain at this time does the greatest possible injury to the crop. The strength and pungency of the leaf is then washed away, and the leaf deteriorates and sells at a low price.

When the plants have acquired a moderate height, the clusters of small leaves that grow at the base of the branches are torn off, but not thrown away. They are dried in the sun and then sold to tobacconists at a much lower price than the better sort of tobacco leaves. These last, as we have said before, are cut in January and dried in the air in some shady places,—generally in the cowshed. This slow process of dressing is said to improve the quality of the tobacco. Very often they are smoked for a considerable time before they are sold. When they are perfectly dry, but not crisp, they are rolled up in bales and sent by cart or boat to markets for sale.

Date trees. There are two kinds of *gur* or molasses manufactured in our villages, the one being produced from date juice, the other from sugarcane. Date trees are generally planted at random without apparently any choice of land. After the trees have grown up they annually yield juice in winter without any labor on the part of the grower.

Abut the beginning of November every year date trees are tapped, and earthen pots are tied to the tree, so that the juice issuing from the portion that is cut may fall into the vessel. The juice issues only in the night, and every morning the vessels are taken down and emptied and then tied to the trees again. Thus every tree yields juice for months together every year, and so for thirty, forty, or fifty years. The juice thus collected is boiled in large cauldrons for a considerable time, the date leaf being used as fuel. When the watery substance has evaporated and the juice has thickened and diminished in quantity it is poured into small earthen vessels where it cools and congeals and becomes *gur*. Date *gur* is not an article of foreign trade, but is extensively used for local consumption. Date trees cease to yield juice on the approach of the summer season.

Sugarcane.—Sugarcane is planted about the end of March, and the plants are cut about the end of January. Considerable care is bestowed on the cultivation of the sugarcane. The land is ploughed deep and manured with oil-cakes and refuse before the seed is sown. After the seeds are sown rain is required, and if the rains fail, artificial irrigation is resorted to.

The process of making *gur* from the sugarcane is much the same as the manufacturing of *gur* from the date juice. The cane is cut into small pieces and thrown into a rude sort of machine, which turns round, and the juice comes out. The juice is then boiled and poured into vessels where it cools and congeals.

We have spoken of *gur* or molasses only and not of sugar, as this last is manufactured not in villages but in towns.

Indigo, like *Aush* dhan, is sown in April and reaped in September.* Indigo grows best on alluvial soil, and

* In *chars* however, and banks of rivers, indigo is sown at the end of autumn, when the waters of the rivers have just receded and left them dry. The reaping of such indigo takes place somewhat early,—say in July or August, *i. e.*, before the great rivers have swollen with the annual rains and deluged such banks and *chars*. In years of heavy rain-fall, the reaping in such places is hurried on, and immature plants have to be cut, and the yield therefore is scanty.

for this reason *chars* and river banks are selected. The manufacturing of indigo requires some skilled labor. The plants are cut and carried to factories and put into vats, into which water is pumped and the plants are left to rot. The water in the vats becomes gradually dyed, and when the proper time comes the plants are thrown away, and the water carefully strained out. The substance which is deposited and remains in the vats (then in a liquid state) is collected and boiled in large cauldrons and cooled in wooden boxes. As the watery matter is not got rid of quickly, these boxes are pressed hard and dried. After the indigo is thus dried, it is cut into cubic cakes and packed up in boxes.

Indigo is a most important article of commerce and is shipped to Europe in large quantities.

From the foregoing it will appear, that some capital is necessary for the production of indigo, and the actual cultivators of the soil therefore can never produce indigo themselves. They generally find employment with planters who advance them capital and seed for the growing of indigo, and after the crops are reaped employ them in the factories in the making of indigo. European planters and companies of planters are to be found almost all over Bengal owning large tracts of land which produce indigo, and producing and annually exporting large quantities of indigo to Europe and elsewhere. Such planters, living in the heart of the country and in remote sub-divisions and villages, have done much good to the country. They construct roads, clear jungles, encourage trade and extend the limits of cultivation. With much that is good, however, they used, and still use to do much that is reprehensible. The prestige of the British name was prostituted by self-seeking planters for the furtherance of their own interests; and violence and coercion of the most reprehensible character used to be resorted to to compel ryots to produce indigo, or labor in the indigo fields and factories. Fifteen years ago this sort of oppressiveness of the great Bengal Indigo Company of Nuddea called forth a loud protest from the people in the shape of a general rebellion, and the Company failed in consequence. Such oppressiveness however has greatly decreased latterly, and is in these days practised by the subordinate servants and retainers often unknown to their European masters.

A very large number of Hindu and Mussalman zomindars have now turned Indigo planters and have taken to producing the commodity in a smaller scale. It is believed that the cultivation of indigo is thus daily increasing. Such small zemindars have not the power to be oppressive or to coerce ryots in any respect; but, on the other hand, they are found sadly wanting in that enlightened interest which every European planter takes in the condition of the country and the people.

Silk. Silk too is largely produced by European factors in many parts of the country. The people of entire villages are sometimes .employed by such factors in the growing of mulberry plants and generally in the preparation of silk. Advances are made to each individual ryot at the beginning of the year for the cultivation of mulberry plants, and after the plants are grown and the cocoons gathered, the able-bodied men of entire villages are often seen assembled together and find employment in the big factory of the silk-producing company. The power which the factors possess over the population of such villages is necessarily very great, and we wish we could say it is never grossly abused.

Petty capitalists too in silk-producing districts very largely employ their capital in the production of silk, but the silk so produced is generally inferior in quality to that produced in European factories. So much has been written on the subject of the growing of silk that we need not say a word about it.

Cotton. There are two sorts of cotton grown in this country, the *simul* and the *karpas*. There is no such thing as regular *simul* cultivation,—the big trees grow here and there at random and give out cotton in the month of Chaitra year after year, the same tree yielding cotton for many years. *Karpas,* on the other hand, is regularly sown and grown on lands cultivated for the purpose. The seed is sown at the time of the Aush sowings in Baisakh, and the young plants thrive with rain, and yield cotton in winter in Pous and Magh. Generally *karpas* is sown annually, but some *karpas* plants yield cotton for more than one year. The *simul* cotton is mostly used in making cushions, beddings, &c., while the *karpas* makes thin *leps*, and is extensively used for making thread for weaving cloth.

Cotton is largely exported to Europe, and is also used in the making of indigenous clothes, &c. Cotton is taken to *hats* and markets and bought by poor village women who make thread out of it and sell it at a very trifling profit. At one time cotton-spinning was the chief occupation of most village women, and specially widows, but in the present days the thread and fabrics imported from Manchester are so much cheaper and better than what is produced at home that the home products fail to find an adequate market, and both spinning and weaving have much decreased in late years,—thereby inflicting a serious loss on the weaver castes of Bengal. Some of our countrymen deplore this as an unmitigated evil, but judging impartially we are bound to say that the benefits derived greatly preponderate the evil. The evil concerns only one particular class, *viz.*, the weavers, and also to a very small extent those women who used to derive some profit from spinning. In any European country the evil would not have been felt, in as much as the weaver capitalists on finding their trade unprofitable would at once have turned their capital to more lucrative manufactures; but in a country like Bengal, where custom is the law of the land and weavers are weavers not by choice but by birth and cannot soon choose a different profession, the evil no doubt is long felt. But the benefits derived are national and universal,—the titled Raja, the respectable Government servant, the village mahajan and gomushta, the plodding ryot, *all* get better clothing at a cheaper price. In this respect there has been quite a change within the last 20 years; respectable but poor people have found a great relief and dress much more decently at a cheaper cost than formerly by taking to Manchester *dhutis* and long-cloth; and even the ryots, without laying out a penny more in clothing, are less scantily clothed in summer, and more comfortably provided in winter than in former days. When the benefits are so tangible and so widespread, it requires some hardihood to deplore the trading power of Manchester, by dwelling on the undoubted misfortune of one particular class of people. Undoubtedly the most advantageous course for India would be for her to import machines, and so manufacture cheap fabrics in India, and dispense with the services of Manchester. Our capitalists cannot do a greater good to the country, or employ their capital in a nobler way, than by importing such machines and manufacturing cheap fabrics. Apart from the fact that such attempts will give ample employment to indigenous labor, and enable the nation to buy cheaper clothing than what even Manchester furnishes us with, there is a still higher interest at stake. It is by improved manufacturing skill and energy alone, and not by feeble attempts to master a foreign literature and language that we can ever hope to rise in the scale of nations.

Note.—We make no apology in extracting the following admirable paper on the Agriculture of Bengal, said to be from the pen of Mr. Seton Karr, from the columns of the *Indian Economist.*

"To break up the clay or loam of Bengal, dried and baked by months of sun, to keep up the village reservoirs to their proper fulness, to prevent the smaller streams from running dry, to give the late rice plants that depth of water which converts a vast plain into one huge wet field of unbroken cultivation, and to enable the higher lands to produce two successive and distinct crops in one twelve-month, some sixty to eighty inches of rain are almost indispensable. But Bengal, and indeed India generally, must have, to use a Biblical expression, the former and the latter rain in due season. The prospects of the finest year may be hopelessly ruined if the showers are not vouchsafed to the land at due intervals and with occasional breaks of sunshine. If an undue proportion of wet is gauged in May and June, the ryot cannot sow the best and deepest lands, or he sows them late and in haste, for the seed to rot or the young plants to be drowned. If the return of the periodical rains is delayed beyond the middle of June, the same result occurs: and before the rice can gather head, as it were, it is overtopped by a deluge in July and August, when the windows of heaven are sometimes opened for a week in succession. On the other hand, it is quite possible that every thing may go on well till the middle of September. The rice sown on both high and low lands in May and June, strengthened but not overwhelmed by the heavier downfall of August, after a week or ten days of sunshine in September, just wants several good inches of rain to keep the roots wet while the ear is developed. But the clouds hold off or do not dissolve; and the richest hopes are converted to blank despair by the mere omission of half-a-dozen inches at the close of September or the beginning of October. In fact, it is perfectly possible to conceive a scarcity with seventy inches of rain all confined to June, July, and August, and a year of unusual abundance with fifty inches distributed in timely and successive falls between the first of June and the 15th or 20th of October. Perhaps the happiest distribution is when there is never more than a fortnight or three weeks of sunshine without rain during that period, and the worst is when all the supply is exhausted before the middle of September. Better that the dry heat of May should be prolonged till the middle of July than that moisture should cease at the very time when the rice-stalks are two and three feet in length. In the years 1844, 1848, 1851, and 1858, Bengal was saved by a timely downfall which occurred at various dates in October. In the first mentioned year, the whole country exchanged dearth for plenty or escaped a famine by 3 days of rain, which began, at the very nick of time on the 11th of October. This is exactly what has been prayed for this season by editors and statesmen, by prophets and planters, by Brahmins and Sudras, and what has not been given.

Broadly speaking, the lands of Bengal and Behar including, of course, all the threatened districts, may be divided into two classes, the higher and drier lands which produce two crops in the year, and the deep-low-lying tracts which are only fitted for rice. Though some divisions are more subject to inundation than others and retain sheets of water for eight months out of the twelve, yet both kinds of land are constantly found in the same village and in one and the same plain.

A few inches more or less of earth, a greater or less incline or outfall, an exchange of loam for sand, and of vicious clay for loam, will make all the difference between a single and a double crop in the year. Cultivation on the high levels commences in March or April, and the ground is then tilled for rice, pulse, vetches, hemp, oil-seeds, some vegetable, and indigo. In the space of from 90 to 130 days all these crops are sown, grow to perfection, and are cut and carried. No sooner is one crop disposed of than the ground is ploughed for, what is called by Anglo-Indians, the "cold-weather crop." This may be wheat, barley, chick pea (termed gram) the poppy, and the coarser cereals in Behar; oats, barley, gram, mustard, pepper, peas, and vetches in Bengal. These crops, if sown when the ground is still soft and moist in the end of September or October, and if benefited by the parting showers which wind up the rainy season, will do perfectly well without irrigation till they are fit to cut. In Behar, indeed, and in Upper India to a much greater extent, this crop is irrigated by wells and water-courses. In Bengal, we have for years seen splendid breadths of mustard, gram, barley, peas, and pulse, which had very little other moisture than the dews of heaven, from the day the seed was put in the ground in October to the time it was reaped in March. In most years the bright, exhilarating, and not oppressive sun-shine of the cold season is now and then obscured by clouds, and rain generally falls for a couple of days at any time between the middle of December and the middle of February. This visitation has nothing tropical about it. The drops descend pretty much as they do in moderate autumnal showers in England. The crops, if the rain be unaccompanied by hail, look better than ever. Ryots shiver in their scanty clothing of American or Manchester workmanship, and Englishmen encamped in the interior of districts for surveying, inspection, or sport, or for all three combined, draw round an extemporized fire-place, and dream for a day or two that their tents are pitched in Sommersetshire or Cannockchase, instead of by obscure streams and populous villages loftily named after Hindu deities or Mahommedan Nawabs.

The above statement must be understood entirely to apply to high level lands and their crops. The winter or late crop of rice, as it is termed, occupies the land for a period rarely less than 6, often 8, and sometimes even 10 months in the year. The deep, marshy, clayey soil bears this one crop and none other. On it centre the hopes of the ryot, and to it is devoted as much continuity of strenuous exertion as can ever be expected from Asiatic muscles. The great object is to get the ground prepared and a good deal of this rice timely sown in May, June or July, so that the young stalks may not be overwhelmed by a rain-fall in August of 6 or 8 inches in as many hours. Only let the stalks keep their heads above the water, and they shoot upwards with the rising tide, showing that Vishnu, the preserving power in Hindu mythology, is quite capable of coping with Shiva the destroyer. A large portion of this crop is sown broad-cast, is never weeded, and with fine sun-shine above and water below measured by inches and even by feet, turns out in January or February, a fulness of ear and a wealth of straw, which would amaze the most skilful Lothian farmers. We have ourselves counted as many as 376 grains on one stalk, and have plucked stalks twice the length of the tallest of men. But as the rice crops are divided into high and low levels, so there is sub-division of this later crop. In tracts neither too high nor too low, where the water continuously fills the plain to the depth of a few inches or at most a foot, the crop is planted out by hand. It is sown in small nurseries, in places under the close personal inspection of the ryot, and removed to fields carefully ploughed, scraped, weeded, and smoothed, at any time in the months of July and August. While the rice sown broad-cast is rarely weeded, but takes its chance with the lotus and other acquatic plants, that transplanted is kept free from grass vegetation with the most scrupulous care. The importance of the late crop may be estimated from the fact that, if harvested, it alone would feed a province. The early rice may be dried up without inflicting any serious loss on the resources of a division; but a failure of the late rice generally is tantamount to a failure of the cold-weather crop also, which succeeds the early rice. The critical time in India for these two crops, as we have pointed out, is the close of the rains. All turns on their not ending too soon. They may not commence until six weeks after they are due. When they begin they may continue for 3 weeks, rot seeds, sweep away crops, destroy houses, flood the railways, and reduce villages to the condition of inhabited islands in an inland sea. These disasters, however grievous, are confined to certain limits, and even if irretrievable for the time, they leave behind them legacies of silt and water, which are by no means ruinous. But a sky of copper during the month of September, and the failure of the parting gift of a few inches usually bequeathed, as the Hindu thinks, by Indra, the rain god, mean simply scarcity, distress, disease, and famine over an extent of country, out of which the area of Lancashire might be cut without being missed.

To see what this rich alluvial soil can display under the simple ploughs and harrows of a people, who have practised agriculture and nothing else for centuries, we should select two days in the year—the beginning or middle of August, and the beginning of February. At the former date, the rainy season is at its height. The early rice is just ready for the harvest: the late crop is sufficiently far advanced to cover with a green carpet plains of such vast amplitude that the village bounding them on one side seems to those on the other like land on the horizon to mariners at sea. These plains are at this time converted into the best and easiest of highways, and they are traversed for perhaps two months by the boats and skiffs of the planter and the missionary, the policeman, and the post. The dense foliage which shrouds the dwellings of some millions of inhabitants is decked out in the verdure and brilliancy of a second spring. Cattle, no longer at liberty to pasture anywhere, are tethered on the very few spots not occupied with a crop of some kind or other, on the very home-steads or on the sides of the village roads. The air is saturated with moisture, and with the perfume of "heavy-blossomed showers" and "heavy-fruited trees." The small embankments which serve both for landmarks or pathways, overtopped by the ripening or the rising crops, are no longer visible, and the country presents two broad characteristics often for some hundreds of miles. These are long waving lines of tall palms and fruit trees, which are identical with the villages, and watery steppes between where hardly a single acre does not contribute its quota to rent, to consumption, and to exports. The climate to an Englishman is simply detestable; but the sight of the Gangetic delta at such an epoch is one which for completeness of husbandry, intensity of color and luxuriance of crops and vegetation, is not easily matched, and which can never be forgotten. The change in six months, at the commencement of February, is in its way no less striking. The cold-weather crops, not quite ready for the sickle, recall the agriculture of temperate zones; the late rice-crops, in many places borne down by its own weight, lies flat on the earth, or on the top of the water, uninjured, golden, full of promise. Bullock carts, heavy with produce, make their own roads and traverse the plains or skirts the marshes with the most perfect facility. Date trees, cultivated not for their fruit, but for their juice, discharge the material for treacle and sugar in steady flow. Bevies of quail are flushed in the peas and barley; snipe swarms everywhere in the rice-fields; and ducks in myriads darken the lakes and ponds, or any places where water still lies deep. The weather, though soon to be exchanged for drying winds and clouds of dust, leaves nothing to wish for or grumble at. The zemindars are secure of their rent. The ryots have only the prospect of harvesting the last crop of the agricultural year, and will have no more hard work to do till April, and few instalments of rent to pay before June. Englishmen are compressing as much as possible of active open-air-work and enjoyment intó the remainder of the cold season, fleets of native craft, under no apprehensions of cyclones or tornadoes pierce the great and small arteries of the country, the last batch of magnificent merchant vessels has just left, or is leaving the Hugly; and, considered either from an official, a social or a mercantile point of view, the Gangetic plains put on their best aspect, and display the most palpable evidence of their agricultural wealth." * * * * * *

CHAPTER VII.

TAXATION.

The empty exchequer, the beggared ryot,

I. C. DUTT.

The want of a correct and intimate knowledge of the habits, feelings and sympathies of the people of India, often displayed by her rulers, is certainly singular as it is deplorable. Old Anglo-Indians, ripe with years of hard work and constant cares, return to their quiet English villas, often with curious notions of a people, among whom they have passed the best portion of their life. And, as if by a sad fatality, it sometimes happens, that it is precisely those Englishmen who fill the highest offices in this country, and on whose conduct depends the welfare of the people, that are least intimately acquainted with the real wants of the country. It is not, therefore, a matter of surprize that laws, detrimental to the welfare of the people, are often enacted with the best of intentions.

This singular state of things is, to a certain extent, brought about by the sort of delegated government under which we live. India is to the Englishman a field of his enterprize and a temporary scene of his labors. He is no settler in this country, and, unlike the Mahommedan settlers in India, he does not mingle with the people, does not familiarize himself with their language, their manners, their institutions. His connexion with India altogether ceases on the day when he leaves India for good; and, therefore, even during his tenure of office and power in this country, he still turns towards England as his home, feels like an exile, and looks forward to the quiet retirement of an English home as the reward of a life of cares and troubles. An exile's sympathies with the native population can hardly be strong, and the best disposed of Englishmen do not *feel* the necessity of seeking out the wants of the people of India.

This want of sympathy between the rulers of India and her people has been productive of lamentable results. It has prevented our countrymen from ever imitating, or even appreciating, the virtues and civilization of Englishmen; it has almost necessitated frequent mistakes, and often serious mistakes, in English legislation in India; and, what is worse, it has, in numerous instances, subjected the motives of our rulers to gross misrepresentation; and consequently, that confidence and credit—at least for honesty of intentions—which an enlightened Government and an enlightened people rightly deserve, have often been withheld from the British Government in India even by the educated portion of our countrymen.

But it is not of these evil effects that we now intend to speak. We shall confine our remarks to the mistakes committed with regard to taxation. We shall see that, through want of an intimate acquaintance with the people of India, taxes have been imposed which would have answered very well in England, for several reasons, and which, for the self-same reasons, may be, and have frequently been, converted into engines of oppression in India. And now, we have only to premise, that the present chapter will have reference only to the taxes imposed in the country-parts, and paid by cultivators and villagers.

The distinction between *direct* and *indirect* taxes as pointed out by Political Economists is, that tho former is ultimately paid by the same person who advances the sum to the Government, the latter is advanced by one person but is ultimately paid by another. An income tax, which is a direct tax, is ultimately paid by the same person who pays the money in the first instance, but a tax on the production of indigo is only advanced by the producer, who ultimately indemnifies himself by selling indigo at an advanced price ; so that the real payer of the tax is another person,—he who buys indigo for his own use. The main difference between the effects of direct and indirect taxation is, that the tax-payer, in the former case, *feels* that he pays the tax ; in the latter, he often makes the payment without perceiving it. The payer of the income tax *knows* that he pays the tax, while the payer of the tax on the production of indigo, *i. e.*, the consumer who buys the indigo at an increased price, confounds the tax he pays with the cost of production of indigo, and is hardly aware that any portion of the price, at which he buys the commodity, goes towards the payment of a tax,—in other words that he is paying a tax at all.

The principal objection against direct taxation is, that it is of a harassing nature, and troubles the tax-payer very much. It is a claim on the part of the Government, which can neither be refused nor even delayed ; and the payment of a claim of so peremptory a nature often involves a very great degree of hardship to poor people. The burden of an indirect tax may often be lessened by denying one's-self the luxury of purchasing a thing. The payment of a tax on cotton may be delayed by a poor man persisting in wearing his old clothes, and the payment of a tax on bricks may be deferred by living in the old dilapidated house; but there is no deferring or delaying the payment of a direct tax. The Income tax, the House tax, &c., must be paid down as soon as the bill comes forward.

This objection has far greater weight in India than in England. Every one, who has even a tolerable acquaintance with the villages of this country, must have been struck with the remarkable want of prudence and foresight which characterizes the villagers. To make provision for the future is something, which is almost totally unknown among these people, except only with regard to those things which come within the ordinary routine of their agricultural work. In hard times, our villagers borrow as fast as possible, and every year of good harvest and plentiful crops is marked by a more than ordinary amount of expenditure among the villagers, —buying new clothes and utensils, repairing and rebuilding huts, marrying off sons and daughters. Saving money for future wants is unknown, nor are the reasons far to seek. Never was there a time in Bengal when the ryots could reasonably expect to enjoy to-morrow what they saved today. The complete subordination in which they were held by the zemindars,—their eternal dependence on the Mahajans, the impossibility in olden times of obtaining justice against the strong man who chose to extort, the very imperfect security against offences against property in those days and the almost periodical devastation by internal or external enemies or predatory races;—all these made *saving* out of the question;—all these have made the ryot the careless, improvident being that he is.

This is what makes the payment of a periodical direct tax so trying to the Indian cultivator; for making provision for such payments presupposes a degree of prudence which he does not own. It is this want of prudence which makes him so often look aghast when the Government claim comes forward;—it is this which so often necessitates the sale of his home, lands and goods, and causes his ruin. The pressure of an indirect tax is, as we have seen, more gradual, and is therefore far better sustained by such a people.

But there is another and a more serious objection against direct taxes in India. Illegal exactions by tax-gatherers are unknown in England,—they form the inseparable accompaniment of direct taxation in India. That spirit of resistance which is natural to an Englishman, is altogether wanting in this country, and every recipient of power has therefore ample scope for abusing the power lodged with him. We shall not here refer to this or that particular direct tax to illustrate our remarks, for there is not one of our readers who will not be able to call to mind instances to the point. We sincerely hope that the truth,—that harrassing direct taxes can never be imposed on our *villages* without a cruel amount of extortion—has at last been arrived at by our legislators never to be lost sight of. We hope that amid the bustle of a constantly changing sea of legislation, there are some axioms which like the pole star will never be lost sight of by those who wield the helm of this vast country. For the sake of the poor and the cultivators of Bengal we hope that new experiments in direct taxation will never be tried among them.

In what we have said above, we have only sought to establish the truth that, direct taxes, however they may do in towns, will never answer in the villages of Bengal, at least for long years to come. When the peasantry of

Bengal will have received as good a practical education as English peasants; when, through the influence of education, they will feel in themselves a power sufficient to repel the cruel claims of the zemindar and the unjust exactions of the tax-gatherer; when it will be possible to estimate, with tolerable ease and accuracy, the incomes of the peasants,—then, and not till then, should such direct taxes, as the Income Tax and the Road Cess, be imposed in the villages. Till then, *indirect* taxes ought to be the main source of revenue in India, so far as the villages are concerned. When Lord Northbrook first came to India, some members of the British Indian Association complained to him about the grievance of the Road Cess. That good-hearted and honest-minded Englishman at once pointed out, that it was not unusual in England to meet local requirements by local direct taxes. His lordship did not pass many months in India, before perceiving the truth and importance of the remark, that "India is not England." England is a rich country,—rich even to over-flowing. The hardships connected with the payment of direct taxes cannot therefore be much felt. In India, such hardships are aggravated by the ignorance and weakness of the people.

On the other hand, the argument most strongly urged by English political economists against *indirect taxation* is, that it takes away money from the hands of the tax-payer without his perceiving it, and therefore affords the Finance Minister too many opportunities for extrava-

N

gance. This argument well becomes a free and prosperous country. In a country, where the people keep a fixed eye on the conduct of the representatives they have chosen to manage public affairs, it is but natural, that the Finance Minister, like all other ministers, should be kept in check; in a land, whereof money there is plenty, it is natural, that the people should be careful that too much is not spent, and that tax should be condemned which affords facilities for excessive expenditure.

Far different is the case in India. Here, the poverty of the people, and not any artificial distinction in the nature of taxes, ought to be the safeguard against extravagant expenditure. And the deplorable poverty of the people should be taken into consideration, not only in fixing the amount of expenditure, but also in determining the nature of taxes. And, if there is any truth or force in the arguments we have already stated, one point has been clearly established, that, with few exceptions, direct taxes in villages are never worth their cost in the ill-feeling which they generate, and the oppression they almost necessitate. On the other hand, indirect taxes are always paid without resistance or grumbling, and often without any knowledge of the payment. Much has been said against such indirect taxes as a tax on tobacco or a tax on salt. But, in our humble opinion, the increased price of tobacco, caused by a tax, would have at least the salutary effect of preventing its too excessive consumption; and salt is so cheap a commodity, that it can easily bear a higher price, without causing much hardship even to the humblest peasant. We do not consider these taxes as by any means the best specimens of indirect taxes that could be imposed on villagers, since we believe they would fall too heavily on the poorer classes as compared to the richer ones; and the first and most important canon in the science of taxation, *viz.*, equality of sacrifices by all classes, would be to a certain extent violated,—unless indeed the equilibrium were maintained by some other tax being imposed exclusively on the richer classes. But even such as they are, those taxes would not cause much hardship, and as substitutes for the Road Cess they would assuredly be hailed with a universal outburst of thanksgiving by the poor villagers of Bengal.

The root of the mistakes relating to taxes lies, however, not in the manner in which they are imposed, but in their amount; and this brings us face to face with a question of vast importance. We feel we are treading on delicate grounds,—but we also feel it our duty unhesitatingly to assert that the crying evil in India is the amount of State Expenditure. The country has been overburdened with impositions,—every tax has been screwed to the sticking point, and yet more money is wanted. The greatest Financier, therefore, of India will be,—not he who will impose new taxes to meet new expenditure,—but he who will cure the radical evil by unmercifully applying the shears to the State Expenditure. We shall venture to offer a few hints as to how they should be applied.

The notoriety which the Public Works Department has obtained for its extravagance, induces us to begin with that department. The complaint that the department spends too much is general, but the proportion which the total of such expenditure bears to the revenue of the country was never more ably exhibited than in the lucid exposition of that subject by Lord Mayo. Very rightly he included under the head of Public Works not only the expenditure directly spent on them, but also grants and guarantees to private companies engaged in constructing railways, canals and ports in India. Lord Mayo says:*—"I wish the Council to note these facts, because I do not believe that it is generally known, that there is such an enormous expenditure going on for works of public utility. If we put these two sums together, we shall have expended in the two years ending March 31, 1871, upon works of public utility and their cognate expenses, altogether the enormous sum of 28½ millions, a sum considerably more than the annual revenue either of Spain, of Italy, of North Germany, and three times as much as that of Holland. * * To put it in another way, the net expenditure on public works, deducting recoveries for this year, amounts to £13,800,000 which, compared with the net available

* *Gazette of India*, 9th April, 1870.

revenue, [by available revenue was meant the revenue after deducting all imperative charges such as cost of collection, pensions, payment of interest &c.,] gives a sum equal to 47 per cent. This percentage will be increased during the present year; so that in reality we expect to spend within the ensuing year, on works of public utility in India, a sum nearly equal to half our entire available revenue; and I believe that *this is an effort in the direction of public improvement that has hardly ever been attempted by any other nation in the world.*" The italics are our own. Now, we have to ask in all fairness, whether the resources of a poor country are equal to such fabulous expenditure. We appeal to the good sense of a well-meaning Government, whether, while tax upon tax is heaped on the shoulders of a groaning nation, while the strain on our finances has raised a cry of dissatisfaction all over the British empire, the Public Works Department should be allowed to spend millions after millions on objects which, under the present circumstances, had better remain unattempted. We do not object to vast expenditures on really useful objects; —in the next chapter we shall have occasion to advocate such expenditures for the prevention of famines; what we complain of is the frequent expenditure of public money or things that are not urgently needed,— or on edifices which threaten to tumble down within a year after they are built.*

* The numerous "buildings that fall down before they are finished or shortly after completion and have to be reconstructed, are called by those who have the heart to joke upon such subjects, *reproductive works.*"—PRITCHARD'S paper on *Indian Finance.*

To remedy this state of things, as well as to provide that money may not be uselessly or extravagantly spent, it has been proposed by Sir Bartle Frere, "that Parliament should pass an Act appointing a Commission, or Trustees, who should have power to raise and apply a large sum of several millions sterling; this sum to be raised by loan in England, the interest to be paid by the Secretary of State for India in Council from the revenues of India, and the money to be applied to public works in India." * This would no doubt be a very salutary measure, if we could feel certain that it would induce the British public and the British Parliament to mark, with a careful and even with a jealous eye, the way in which the money so raised is spent in India. But where is the security for that? Where is the security that English capitalists, secure of their fixed rate of interest obtainable from the Indian Government, would not be totally unmindful as to how the money is spent? Sir Bartle's plan does not provide a sufficient check on the conduct of the Trustees; and without such checks, public bodies in India are invariably apt to be extravagant. We believe a far simpler and a more efficient plan would be, to somehow create a direct personal responsibility in India. The Finance minister might be made directly responsible to the Government of India for not sanctioning over a *fixed sum* of some millions sterling annually for Public Works in India. Out of

* Sir BARTLE FRERE's paper on *Public Works in India.*

this fixed sum, a margin,—say a fourth, might be left for any emergent items of expenditure which might spring up during the course of the financial year, and could not be anticipated. The remaining three-fourths should be distributed at the beginning of the financial year among the different proposals of public works, submitted by the local Governments before the close of the previous year. Thus the local Governments should submit before the close of the year, proposals and estimates of public works to be constructed during the next year; and the imperial Government should sanction or reject such proposals, after considering their importance and the state of the finances, and *on no occasion should the fixed sum above referred to be exceeded.* It would require some moral courage to consistently follow out such a policy, and to reject hundreds of proposals which crop up every year, entailing increased expenditure on public works; but Indian officials have never been found wanting in courage in times of need, and the present head of our Government has never hesitated a refusal when a refusal was needed.

We have done with the Public Works Department, but there is one thing which we cannot pass over without remark,—we mean the policy of guaranteeing profits to private companies, which has been consistently followed by the Government, and which tells most detrimentally on the finances of India. The loss which the Government, or rather the tax-payers, have already sustained is enormous,* and yet there seems to be no immediate prospect of the policy being given up. The failure of companies has always, and in every country, called forth the sympathy of the people, but nowhere have the people been taxed to prevent it. The failure of Railway companies is a frequent occurrencee in England, but the English Government has not in any single instance ventured to indemnify the sufferers by a tax on the people. We fail to see why a different policy should hold in India.

One of the principal evils resulting from such guarantee systems is that it makes the parties concerned unmindful of the ways in which profits might be increased. The Indian Government has had several occasions

* "Up to the present time about £90,000,000 has been spent on guaranteed railways; the amount of interest which the Government has had to make good up to the present time has been £33,000,000. The contracts are arranged on conditions most unfavourable to India. Government can at any time be compelled to take over a company repaying to the share-holders not only the actual value of the line, but also all the capital that has been wasted on ill constructed works. Upon the Calcutta and South Eastern Railway about £600,000 was expended. On this outlay 5 per cent was guaranteed. The scheme proving a disastrous failure, the Government took it over at par, and it does not now nearly pay its working expenses. £3,000,000 was expended on the Jubbulpore Branch of the East Indian Railway. The usual 5 per cent was guaranteed, and it only just pays its working expenses. Other still more disastrous instances might be quoted. In Scinde, Punjab and Delhi Railway more than £8,000,000 was expended, upon which 5 per cent has been guaranteed. The net annual return at the present time is about £50,000, and the Government annually loses about £40,000 on this disastrous undertaking. The share-holders however are perfectly happy. They are certain of their 5 per cent.—FAWCETT's Speech on *Indian Finance.*

to warn the Railway Companies to treat native passengers and traders with courtesy. Had such warnings been needed if the companies had not been secure of their profits?

It might be urged in defence of the conduct of the Indian Government, that English capitalists would not venture on risking their money in this distant land without some security for the interest of their capital. To such as would bring forward this argument we would simply ask,—Is not English capital finding its way into the heart of Russia, into the wilds of Australia, into the trackless woods of America,—and that without any security whatever being afforded? Is not English capital running greater risks in every other part of the world than in India? Nay, it is a notorious fact, that the excess of accumulation in England leads to commercial revulsions, and therefore necessitates, almost periodically, the destruction of vast amounts of English capital, in order to the maintenance of a healthy rate of profits in the market. Why then should any security be needed in India?

We have dwelt so long on this subject that we must hurry over the remaining points. Perhaps the most popular, and in our opinion, the wisest measure, by which retrenchment might be effected would be the employment of a larger number of the natives of the country in Government offices. No Government perhaps on the face of the globe is so expensive as the

Indian Government; and the pay of the Indian officials of the higher grades is almost unparalleled by that of any other nation. If English talent cannot be bought at a more reasonable price, does not the state of the finances necessitate the recognition and a more extensive use of indigenous talent and abilities? We do not certainly object to the English taking every possible measure to provide for the security of British power in India, but we do think that such security is perfectly compatible with according a larger share in the administration of the country to its native inhabitants. We are stating our simple conviction in saying that British Power in India would be rather strengthened by allowing Indians to fill high and honorable posts under Government which are now kept as a monopoly for Englishmen. Such a measure may well be calculated to make British Government in India cheaper, and at the same time far more popular than what it is in the present day.

But should the English be overscrupulous on this point,—should they consider the retention of all or almost all executive power, as indispensible for the maintenance of British power in India, we can still point to other offices which have nothing whatever to do with the administration of the country; and to such offices our countrymen should certainly be allowed to aspire. We do not see how the opening up of the educational service to the natives of the country can in any conceivable degree diminish British power in India. An Englishman will always make the best professor in English; but we do think a Mahommedan professor of Mathematics or a Hindu professor of Philosophy, a Hindu or a Mahommedan Director of Public Instruction will, with his intimate knowledge of the country and the people, actually do his duties better than an Englishman of equal talent and abilities. Superintendents in different departments, accountants, engineers, registrars, &c., might with advantage be selected from the native population of Bengal. We are aware, such measures would disturb a nest of hornets. A hue and cry will be raised by the educational and other services, but we do not know how far the Government of India will be justified in keeping up a uselessly prodigal system of expenditure in compliance with such cry.*

---

* "We know that the Mogul emperors employed without hesitation the talents of their Hindu subjects both in finance and in war, and that more than one province was brought under obedience to Delhi by the abilities of a Hindu General. Could we not take a lesson from such precedents? * * Whatever prejudices may linger in Anglo Indian breasts, the feeling of the nation at home is that India should be governed not only for the benefit of the people but also by their own leaders so far as is consistent with the stability of the administration."—*Times.*

"'Could we not' asks the *Times* 'take a lesson from such precedents'? Of course we can if we only have the courage to carry out our own professions of governing India for the good of the people. It was not by employing Native Hindus but by ceasing to employ them that the Mogul Empire came to grief."—*Home News.*

"In many respects the Mahommedans surpassed our rule; they settled in the countries which they conquered—the interests and sympathies of the conquerors and conquered were identified. Our policy, on the contrary, has been the reverse of this—cold, selfish, unfeeling. The iron hand of power, on the one side, monopoly and exclusion on the other."—LORD WILLIAM BENTINCK's *Minute.*

We have neither the space nor the heart to go over the details of State Expenditure item by item, and shall therefore hurry on to a close. Our acquaintance with the army expenditure is so slight that what we might say on the subject, would be trite. All accounts however agree in representing a portion at least of the standing army as extremely inefficient, and the money spent on it as almost literally spent in vain. They further agree in exposing the extravagance of the Commissariat department; and we have hopes Government will take steps to remedy the existing state of things.

There is one subject however which we cannot pass over, and that is the Christian Church Establishment in India. From time to time the injustice of maintaining a Christian church at the cost of a non-Christian population has been mooted, but with little effect, and the prospect of the Christian church in India being disestablished is, yet, as hopeless as ever. And yet the injustice of taxing the people of India for churches from which they derive no benefit is so marked that it needs no comment. We hope we shall not be mistaken. We do not for a moment declare that we have received no benefits from those who come to preach Christianity among us. The services of Dr. Duff for education in India, the services of Rev. J. Long for the good of the people are indeed invaluable. But we want our readers distinctly to understand that it is precisely for such services that we do not pay a penny—it is simply for weekly sermons, delivered before Englishmen mostly, that we are taxed as a nation. The good that the missionary Dr. Duff has done to India has] been done *gratis*, the good that missionaries do in the heart of wild tracts is all done *gratis*. For his sermons in a church in Calcutta Rev. Long was paid,—for his heroic struggle to save a voiceless people from fearful extortions and oppression, Rev. Long was fined and imprisoned.

In a parallel instance Englishmen have admitted the injustice of maintaining a religion at the expence of a nation which does not profess such religion;—in that case however, other causes were at work. The loyalty and the peaceful habits of the people of India preclude the possibility of such incentives springing up in India as induced English statesmen to disestablish the church in Ireland; but, in our humble opinion, the critical state of our finances, and the hardships to which our villagers have been subjected on account of the daily increasing taxation, ought to be a sufficient incentive in the present instance,—if indeed any incentive is necessary for the disestablishment of an institution which is admitted to be uujust.

As our remarks in this Chapter have been somewhat disconnected, we shall here recapitulate. We have shewn that, as a rule, direct taxation is utterly unsuited to the condition of things prevailing in our villages, and is almost certain in every case to give rise to cruel extortions as well as hardships, since a ryot is almost always improvident, and never prepared to meet a sudden demand. The Road Cess Act seems to take cognizance of this fact, and enacts that ryots should pay to their zemindars, as zemindars always know how to suit their demands to the convenience of the ryots. But how heavily do the ryots pay for this little concession. As tax-gatherers the zemindars are about the very worst people that could have been chosen,—and cases have come to light in which the ryots paid four annas instead of a pice per rupee!

We have also shewn that the radical defect to be cured lies in the enormous extent of State expenditure. The Public Works Department has a bad reputation, and is not improperly called the Public Waste Department! It is a most startling fact,—and yet fails to startle us because it is a daily and hourly occurrence, that officers employed in this department on, say, a hundred rupees per mensem, often succeed, after two or three years' service, to buy up zemindaries, or build up big houses; and the nation is systematically impoverished to enrich these dregs of society! And lastly we have pointed out a variety of other ways in which Financial Reforms may be effected.

Note.—We have said in the foregoing chapter that a tax which may be perfectly suited to the habits and conditions of life in England may be unsuitable in India. We shall here try to illustrate our views with an instance. English political economists agree in considering the House Tax as one of the very best that could be imposed on a people. In London and all other English towns people live mostly in hired houses and apartments,--just as Englishmen do in India. The active habits of a nation of travellers and traders and colonists are opposed to the system which prevails in our own country of generations together leading a stationery sort of life in the same patriarchal house. Civilized notions of convenience too prevent an Englishman from building anything like a *hereditary* building, which his son or successor in altered circumstances may find too large or too small, too rich or too poor for his position,—or withal not situated in the part of the town in which he may choose to live. Whatever may be the reasons, the fact remains that in English towns most or all people live in hired houses and apartments. A person who lives in a hired house has not any strong motive to stick to it, and often for the sake of comfort or convenience or even for whim or a change, he changes his residence. It follows that every change in the circumstances of a person is followed by a change of place; and as a rule the sort of house or apartments in which a person lives in England is *always* a fair index of his circumstances and position in life. And the primary canon of taxation being to make every man pay according to his circumstances, it follows that a more judicious tax in English towns could not be invented than a tax on houses,—for such a tax would almost in every particular case be suited to the circumstances of the rate-payer.

In India the case is different. We have already spoken of the hardship attending direct taxation which is more felt in India than in England. But house taxes are liable to yet further objections. For a variety of reasons, it is a custom with the people of this country to build up *hereditary* houses. The stationary life which the homeloving Bengali always lived and yet lives, has given rise to this custom ; while the insecurity of life and property which always prevailed here before the coming of the English no doubt further developed the system of investing money in houses and buildings which could neither be stolen by thieves nor taken away by robbers. From a variety of causes then has risen a custom which we still observe of living in the same hereditary house for generations together. The impoverished descendant will continue to occupy his ancestor's splendid apartments, and a man of newly acquired wealth will for years continue to live under the poor parental roof. Such being the case the anxiety to build up houses for descendants rather than for one's self is proportionately great, and nothing is more common than to find men investing their *whole* property in building up a sort of cover under which they fondly hope their sons and grandsons will find shelter for generations to come. This longing is specially observable in villages. Poor Brahmins who have a few acres of Brohmottor land, and get hardly enough to keep body and soul together, will yet build up pucka permanent buildings. How do they manage it? In a year of gold harvest they spare something to make a few thousand bricks. Another such year adds to their number. He fells some of his old trees and manages to burn the bricks and get beams and doors made. He borrows something from a mohajan and builds up a room. Years pass on and another room is added. Before he dies he thus manages to leave some sort of convenient shelter for his children. Such is the way in which a poor man in our country builds up his only hereditary wealth, and when the tax-gatherer tells him, that the possession of a pucka house implies, and is an index to, good circumstances, the poor house-owner who has felled his own trees, dug his own earth, borrowed dhan of the mohajan and money of the zemindar to build his house, has indeed strong reasons to gape with terror and wonder.

A house-tax, then, is liable to two objections in Bengal. In the first place a house is not always a fair index to the circumstances of the resident,—poor men often living in big ancestral houses, and rich men in comparatively small houses ; and secondly a house of a given quality and proportions implies less wealth in its owners than the same sort of house would do in other countries. For the first reason house-taxes should be avoided wherever it is possible to do so, for the second reason they should be collected with extreme moderation and care where they cannot possibly be avoided. Municipal taxes have made living in Calcutta extremely difficult to men of limited means; and the Road Cess on houses would have had the same cruel effect in villages but that Sir George Campbell imposed it with extreme leniency, and thereby exempted from its operation by far the majority of such villages and persons as might have been compelled to pay it by law.

CHAPTER VIII.

FUTURE PROSPECTS.

'Tis man, and man alone, ignobly sleeps—
Sleeps in the shadow of those ruins stern!
* * * * *
Must this inglorious sleep for ever last
And last on Gunga's sacred shores alone?

S. C. DUTT.

WE have finished our short review of the past and present condition of the Bengal peasantry, and shall in this last chapter make a few observations on their future prospects. We shall rapidly go over the circumstances which have influenced the character of the people, and shall then examine in how far such circumstances have been affected or altered by British administration in India.

The manner in which the soil and climate of this country influence the character of the people, must be apparent even to the most superficial observer. All those physical causes which enfeeble and enervate, and make man incapable of having mastery over Nature, are found to exist and work in this country to an alarming extent. The damp heat of Bengal, unlike the dry heat of western India, disposes the people to be inactive and averse to labor; while the alluvial soil of the land, moistened and softened by periodical rains and innundations, produces an exuberance of crops almost without the toil of man, and denies him that salutary physical exercise which is necessary in more hilly countries. Rice too, which is the chief produce of the land, affords nourishment rather than strength.

All these causes have acted with combined force on the physique of the Bengali, and have made him the weak and inactive creature that he is.

But this is not all. While such influences have made man singularly powerless, Nature and Natural forces, in this country, are pre-eminently strong; and the task of getting the mastery over Nature, and of bringing under human control her endless resources, has ever appeared a hopeless one, to the people of Bengal. Nursed by overwhelming floods and a burning sun, the animal and vegetable life in India, has attained a power nowhere exceeded on the face of the globe. Mighty forests and trackless woods, extending over hundreds of miles, swamps and malarious lakes teeming with rank vegetable and animal life, tigers of the strongest and fiercest description, serpents of the deadliest poison, poisonous reptiles and insects that defy the pains of the naturalist,—these are the primeval dwellers of the soil, and in the pride of their undiminished strength still present to the weak race, that inhabit the land, a formidable front. The furious hurricanes too, devastating villages and entire districts, and the majestic Ganges ever busy in washing away and again re-forming hundreds and thousands of acres, and not unfrequently sweeping away entire villages in her imperious pride, are foes not easy to be conquered by man.* In many places, entire districts are annually inundated by rivers for several months, and the people have to live on *máchans*, putting up with the greatest conceivable inconvenience. In countries where Nature is less violent, man learns slowly to bring under his control her endless resources, but the case is quite otherwise in such a country as this. The terrific convulsions of Nature,

* The vast amount of mischief done by the Ganges is known only to those who have had long experience in the villages. Entire villages on the banks of the Padma are often washed away in the course of one year, and the villagers save themselves only by leaving their homes in time. Even the Bhagirathi washes away from, or adds to, either of its banks thousands of acres year after year.

her sudden and awful freaks, only impress upon man his weakness and utter helplessness, debar him from ever hoping to get the mastery over Nature, and make him timorous, devoid of self-reliance, and superstitious in the extreme.* Utter helplessness on occasions of sudden danger lead to superstition, and excite and develop the imagination to an abnormal extent; and the terrific violence and war of elements in India, the sudden washing away of our villages and the blowing away of our homes, the deadly sting of the unseen serpent, and the fatal spring of the unexpected tiger, the whistling of the gale, and the creaking of trackless woods with their nameless inhabitants,—nay, the very aspect of the huge darksome trees that overshade and almost overawe our villages;—these, combined with our extreme weakness proceeding from physical causes, have filled our skies, or rather our imagination, with three hundred and thirty millions of gods and goddesses, and fairies, fays and elfins, whom we have not yet forgotten to fear and to worship.†

We do not maintain that Nature has always been unkind to us. On the contrary it was through her kindness that we prospered so well during the younger days of our civilization. Every institution in our country seems to be based on the patriarchal system of "good old

---

* Mr. Buckle attributes the superstition of the Spaniards and the Portuguese to the frequent and terrific earthquakes that take place in their country. Read his brilliant chapter on this subject.

† Read Hume's *Phylosophical Essay on Natural Religion.*

times," and we hope we shall not be accused with drawing too much on the imagination if we venture to assert, that the operations of Nature too in this country, since the beginning of our national life, have been in a patriarchal style. The peculiarities which marked the conduct of the *paterfamilias* of the patriarchal times towards his children were, firstly, the extreme care with which he tried to bring them up,—being himself responsible to government for their conduct; and, secondly, the extreme jealousy with which he guarded his own power over them, and prevented them from ever becoming independent.* We shall see how, in both these respects, the operations of Nature in this country resemble the conduct of the typical *paterfamilias*. During the earlier days of our national life, Nature afforded us every facility for the advancement of our civilization. The fertile soil of this country supplied us with plenty of food, and thereby increased and thickened population and facilitated division of labor which is the first requisite for civilization. She gave us a net-work of navigable rivers which, by making communication easy, shortened distance, and further facilitated division of labor among the inhabitants of distant villages. She supplied us, without any effort of our own, with an inexhaustible store of fruits and fish, as well as of vegetable and animal substance for our use. It was through these acts of kindness,—it was on account of these facilities,

* Maine's *Ancient Law*.

that we were enabled to secure for ourselves so early a civilization. We sprinkled our beautiful country with towns and buildings, whose ruins among the trackless woods of the Sunderbunds, or by the shores of the Ganges, still strike the traveller with wonder after the lapse of hundreds of years. We filled our rivers with boats of traffic, we cultivated with success the arts of peace, we cultivated literature, law and metaphysics in our schools of Benares, Tirhoot, Nuddea and other places, with wonderful success ; and we spread over our country practical rules of life and of division of labor, and established customs which have not ceased to work to the present day. But the kindness of *materfamilias*, Nature, ended here. Like children brought up with extreme indulgence, we have never learnt to go beyond her apron strings. As *materfamilias*, she is exceedingly jealous of her power, and has never allowed us to get the mastery over her. We have not learnt to be self-reliant, nor to apply the resources of Nature to our service to any extent worth speaking of. On the contrary, Nature still exercises over us absolute patriarchal authority, and we are still content to view with fear and trembling, but without ever thinking of resistance, her sudden and awful freaks of rage, and the abuse of her absolute power over us.

Far different has been the case with the colder countries of western Europe. Nature (to continue the figure) was to them a *cold*-hearted step-mother, and gave them no facilities for early civilization,—neither fertile soil nor navigable rivers. The people in western Europe, therefore, thus neglected, failed to secure an early civilization. It was later on that they learnt to civilize themselves despite the negligence of Dame Nature, and in that effort to educate themselves they learnt the noble lesson of self-reliance and sustained endeavour, which we have never learnt. These qualities they now employ in a most profitable way, *viz.*, in extorting from Nature (to whom they owe no gratitude) every penny of her vast resources. And in the increasing triumphs of man over Nature, consists the superiority of the civilization of Europe as compared with the civilization of Asia.

We now turn to the historical causes which have influenced the character of the people. The history of Bengal presents us with a universal and cheerless blank so far as the people are concerned. A long and undiversified subjection for gloomy centuries together,—a subjection which we never attempted to get freed from, has combined with the influences of Nature to make us more enervated and dependent. Nature and man combined to impress on our mind the idea of our utter helplessness, and the impossibility of our achieving any thing great by our own endeavour; and we learnt the lesson so thoroughly well, that at last action on any emergent occasion became almost an impossibility with us. Our feelings might be wrought up to the highest pitch without leading us to action, and we could see our homes burnt and our property plundered, with anguish in our heart, but without ever combining for resistance;—indeed, the incursions of the Mahrattas, even like the spread of malarious fevers in Bengal, probably only excited our fears and our imagination, and added to our household gods and goddesses. Since centuries past, therefore, action, on any emergent occasion, has been with us an impossibility, and resistance even to the grossest acts of oppression out of the question. This utter inaction has resulted in oppression being the rule rather than the exception with every recipient of power in Bengal, be he Subadar or Zemindar, Gomasta or Policeman. Utter want of resistance renders power in Bengal liable to abuse to an alarming extent.

Then, again, during the long centuries of Mahommedan rule, and no doubt also during the Hindu rule, which preceded it, security of property was very imperfectly maintained in Bengal. As a natural consequence, foresight and providence for the future among the people was retarded, and accumulation, except in the hands of the rulers, became an impossibility. For, unless there is at least a tolerable certainty of enjoying to-morrow what we keep in store to-day, providence for the future is useless, and is soon dispensed with. And during certain periods in the history of Bengal, specially in the last days of Mahommedan rule, insecurity of property reached its maximum, and indeed almost reached that stage eloquently described by Bentham,* when industry is deadened and the people remain in a torpor of despair. No wonder, therefore, that the peasantry of Bengal have always been remarkable for their improvidence.

The mind turns curiously to enquire into the causes of this state of things. The characteristic features in the history of Western Europe consist in the struggles of the people for independence,—the characteristic feature of Asiatic history is abject and voiceless subjection under kings, potentates or zemindars. Nor are the reasons far to seek. It is the misfortune of warm and fertile countries that, while on the one hand the land produces too much, the producers themselves require too little to supply their natural wants; consequently population increases at a fearful rate, and the wages of labor through the stubborn law of demand and supply decrease to a miserable pittance. While, therefore, much is produced by laborers in such countries, little is consumed by them, and the equitable distribution of wealth is seriously impaired, and undue accumulation in a few hands is fostered to an alarming extent. Hence the phenomenon of isolated lordlings and potentates rolling in wealth and luxury, and surrounded by poor and starving millions, is uniformly presented to the eye by all warm countries with any pretentions to wealth or civilization. In such countries, *national* independence is possible, and is often stubbornly guarded by ideas of

* Bentham's *Theory of Legislation.*

clanship and national union; but as the *individual* counts for nothing, the rights and freedom of *individuals* are unknown and unrecognized. As a nation they may be free, but as men they are subjected to the tyranny of their domestic oppressors. Servility is thus engendered, and all institutions partake of a servile character. On the other hand, in cold countries, while less is produced by the laborers, a large proportion is required for their own sustenance: undue accumulation in a few hands is thus retarded, and the importance and rights of individuals are recognized and respected. True political freedom is therefore maintained in such countries. Every nation has had slowly to progress from a state of utter barbarism. Both starting from the same point, the civilization of Europe has secured for her independent population institutions and a system of distribution of power which recognize and respect individual freedom, while the civilization of Asia has got for her servile children different institutions which ignore the rights of individuals, and give the freest scope to oppression. Even in India, while we find the village communities system prevailing in the North-West, Bengal which is more fertile and enervating than other parts has given rise to the zemindari system which affords the freest scope to oppression.

We shall not here stop to trace how weakness and oppressive subjection smother the noblest feelings of man, and generate some of the worst vices and arts which are the resources of the weak. Nor would our space allow us to trace how many of the remarkable customs in our country have been slowly developed through the influences of natural and historical causes, nor to shew how history itself is the result of natural and physical causes influencing different nations and different bodies of people in different ways. The deeper we go into these investigations the more plainly can we eliminate the phenomena called accidents from the history of nations, and the better can we trace all the general features of history to fixed and unchanging laws. The laws are fixed and immutable, and the only differentiating causes are the different natural influences which produce different effects among nations. But, as we said, we have not time to go into all this. We have said enough to shew how completely the character of the people of Bengal has been moulded by physical and historical causes. It remains for us to consider how these same causes may be expected to operate in future. It may be very pertinently asked why these causes should not operate precisely in the same way in which they have acted so long? What new disturbing element has entered into the scene of action? We answer, that disturbing element is the English civilization with which we have suddenly come in contact;—and we have to consider how this new element, combined with the causes above stated, will act on the character of the people.

The historical causes specified above, which have acted detrimentally on the character of the people, are being removed one by one under the beneficent rule of England. Admitting in its full force the general argument, that subjection in any shape is demoralizing, we still believe we are stating a simple truth when we say, that the sort of *morale* that we had could hardly sink lower, and is fast improving under the mitigated form of subjection we are now under. The freedom of action and even of thought, accorded to us by our rulers, is such as is calculated to revive in us the energy we had entirely lost, and the precepts and example of our rulers are even now instilling into our hearts some degree of assurance and self-reliance. Not the least important service done by British rule in India is the protection afforded to labor and its fruits. The insecure times under the Mahommedan rulers were, as we said before, altogether paralyzing to the active energies of the producers, and snapped the strings of the industry of the nation. For "industry and frugality cannot exist where there is not a preponderant probability that those who labor and spare will be permitted to enjoy. And the nearer this probability approaches to certainty, the more do industry and frugality become pervading qualities in a people."* This security is now afforded by the British government, and trade and accumulation, and the habit of making

* Mills' *Principles of Political Economy.* Book IV. chap. I.

present sacrifices for future gain, are ever on the increase. The education, too, that we are receiving, is every day familiarizing us with the high standard of English morality, and is gradually creating among us a strong enlightened public opinion, which is the best safeguard for the general morality of the people. We have already remarked that the peasantry have come in for a share of these blessings;—and if they have not yet learnt to save,—if they are not yet as prudent, intelligent and provident a set of people as cultivators in happier countries,—they have at least felt their power, and have on occasions exerted it;—and are day by day improving in wealth and education. On these points we intend to dwell at some length.

There is a class of people whom we may designate as utter disbelievers in legislation. They rightly argue that any great improvement in a people must emanate from themselves. They go further, and utterly deny that legislation can ever meterially alter the condition of the people. Mr. Buckle, in his splendid chapters on Spain, has shewn how the wisest and the most liberal legislative measures failed to bring about any improvement in the people during the last century,—because the people were not prepared for it. This very plausible argument is carried a step further, and it is asserted that though by wise legislation and a just administration it is possible to keep peace and encourage trade and agriculture in a country,—to bring about any radical change in the character or condition of the people is beyond the scope of the wisest and best legislation.

There is another class of thinkers whom we may denominate as firm believers in legislation,—a class fairly represented by Sir George Campbell. They seem to suppose it possible to bring about any change and any improvement in the character of the people by a stroke of the pen on the part of the legislators. The attempt to rouse a spirit of co-operation and perhaps freedom by spreading municipalities over the land is an instance in point. Their main idea seems to be that the national character of a people is partly, if not wholly, the result of legislation:—improve legislation and you will improve the character. Unfortunately they ignore the influence of natural and historical causes on the character of nations,—causes which, as we have shewn in the first portion of this chapter, have had such a marked influence in the formation of the character of the people of this country.

Of these two opinions we confess, we accept the former as the sounder,—but we do not accept it altogether. We certainly do not believe that legislation can bring about any desired effect on the character of nations, and like the philosopher's stone of old, turn everything into gold;—at the same time, however, we cannot believe that legislation is utterly useless and has no influence at all. Our own notions on the subject may be neatly expressed in a simile. Legislation in Bengal has and may have the same influence as medicine may be expected to have on the constitution of old men,—it cures maladies and brings on temporary relief,—but it can never, never bring back the pristine vigour and health of boyhood. The wisest and best legislation will not make us a free nation, like the free nations of Western Europe. The spirit of freedom and self-reliance is wanting in us;—such spirit may emanate from within, but can never be imparted by legislation. At the same time there are maladies which English legislation may remove and has removed, and there are subjects on which English legislation may afford us relief. Among the maladies which English legislation,—or rather English education has removed, the oppressive religio-social restrictions of olden days may be mentioned as an important one;—among the reliefs for which we look up to our enlightened Doctor,—the relief, though temporary it may be,—of the peasantry from the servitude of ages is without exception the most important.

We may mention *en passant* that one of the mistakes most frequently committed by hasty legislators is the attempt to renovate old institutions which have had their day of usefulness, and have fairly died out. If history teaches one lesson, it teaches that such institutions can never be artificially created or galvanized into new life by the act of legislators. From the time of Warren Hastings who attempted to revive the Canongoe Duftur system to the time of Sir George Campbell whose desire it was to see the village community system spread through the land, every attempt to revive old systems has been abortive. And the reasons are plain. The action of every institution, as we have remarked before, depends upon surrounding circumstances which are constantly changing. The Panchyet system,—one of the most useful and best that Bengal ever possessed, was a necessity when there were no courts of justice in villages, and even the zemindars who in a rough way supplied the necessity oftener sold than administered justice. At a time, however, when honest and conscien-cious magistrates are to be found within a few miles of every village, it stands to reason that the Panchayet system is no longer a necessity,—and has therefore withered and decayed.

We may also here expose the mistake of those of our countrymen, who in their warm admiration of English institutions believe a close imitation, or introduction into this country, of such institutions as a panacea for all evils. They forget or they ignore the fact that the effect and action of such institutions depend on a thousand and one other circumstances and conditions which like the minute wheels of an engine regulate the action of the machine. Those conditions are far different in this country from what they are in Europe, and an institution productive of good effects in England may have an oppo-site character here. They forget that a cheerful fire is necessary in England, sometimes even in the month of

May or June, but a fire in June in this country will be anything but cheerful. To such we commend the following tale :—A certain Brahman went up from Calcutta to Ulo, and early in the morning went to the river side to perform his morning devotions and ablutions. A damsel who passed that way to the bathing *ghat*, saw the Brahman engaged in making an image of the god Siva from the river-side clay. After some time, while returning from her bath, the girl saw the Brahman still engaged in the same work. "Brahman" ! quoth she, "the sun is up, you have spent the whole morning in making a Siva, when will you worship him and finish your *puja*?" "Damsel !" replied the Brahman, "it is not my fault ; I have been attempting all this time to make a Siva, but such is the soil of Ulo that the figure, despite all my endeavours, invariably turns out to be that of an ape !" We may attempt to import bodily the institutions of England, but such is the soil of our country, that the institutions will too often change their character and turn into veritable apes !

In the previous chapters we have in several places advocated various measures of reform, and pointed out the good that we expect to result therefrom. We shall speak of one or two more before concluding our book. The primary education of the masses and the improvement of the country are among the most important topics of the day.

The much maligned administration of Sir George Campbell in Bengal will ever be associated by future historians with the inauguration of the education of the masses. Hardly any officer has been so severely and, we may say, so unjustly censured by the people of the country as Sir George Campbell, and among his acts hardly any one has been so bitterly censured as his policy of educating the masses of the people. And yet we believe we are stating a simple truth when we say that British Government in India even since the passing of Act X of 1859 has never conceived a more philanthropic measure than the one under consideration. With the exception of the creating of a Permanent Settlement between the ryots and the zemindars, we cannot conceive of a single act which would tend more to the good of the cultivators. The one act would be a sort of complement to the other, the one would lodge power in the hands of the ryots,—for knowledge is power,—and the other would take away power from the hands of their oppressors,—and the two together cannot fail to make the ryot a prudent, self-reliant, calculating, thinking being.

We are fully alive to the importance of the remark often made, that villagers would much prefer employing their sons to help them in their work to sending them to school. We have ourselves heard objections raised by villagers to sending their children to school, so long as those children can be employed in feeding the cows or profitably engaged in silk and indigo factories for 3 Rs.

a month. Nor are we at all hopeful that any extensive use will be made of these village schools during the first few years; on the contrary, it seems exceedingly probable that the villagers will look upon these institutions with suspicion and distrust, even as the Hindu College in its early days was looked upon with distrust by orthodox Hindus. The opposers of Sir George Campbell's measure will therefore have, for some years at least, facts and plausible reasons to congratulate themselves on the wisdom of their anticipations. As, however, the benefit of having one's children educated will become more and more apparent, it is impossible but that the villagers will be impelled by the strong motive of self-interest to make a more general use of the schools, and then the results may be fairly expected to be brilliant indeed.

Nor should we pass over the other argument also brought forward against the primary education of the masses. It is often stated that the children of the cultivators on receiving some sort of education would be discontented with their present low occupation, and would aspire to higher walks of life. Such higher professions, however, being already overcrowded would open no prospect for the new comers, and the whole thing would end in discontent and failure. This argument is based on a fallacious generalization. To be sure, whenever, in an exceptional case, a man belonging to the cultivating classes happens to receive education at the present time, he instantly seeks out for himself some higher walk of life; but does not this happen simply and solely because such cases are exceptional? One village boy receiving education would at once perceive the difference between himself and his ignorant fellow-villagers, and would therefore be tempted to seek what he may consider his proper sphere, but this motive will naturally disappear when a large number of villagers will be educated together. The assertion, therefore, that a wide-spread education of the villagers will be followed by a general desertion by them of their homes and lands (!) and a rush towards the town, contains an eggregious blunder in generalization. Besides, English education is at present so widely spread in every town in Bengal, that an education in reading, writing and arithmetic in the vernacular tongue, such as the late Lieutenant-Governor proposed to bestow on our villagers, will never enable them, even if they were so inclined, to compete with towns. It is evident, therefore, that our villagers with their vernacular education will never aspire to any thing higher than to be honored and respected in their own villages. The zemindars of the country, and the educated people have no doubt little or nothing to gain by the spread of primary education. On the contrary, when the poorest ryot will learn to keep his own accounts, the zemindar's servants will find it more difficult to extort anything of him, and the zemindars themselves will find it difficult to keep at a pay of 2 rupees or 3 rupees per mensem gomashtas whose chances of gain from other sources will be fatally diminished. Are we to suppose that these considerations induced the zemindars to cry out against the measure, that these considerations moved our press,—the representative of the upper ten thousand—to veto the beneficial act with one voice? Never were the true interests of the country so seriously jeopardized by her best educated children.

The improvement of the country is a subject which will occupy the serious attention of our rulers for years to come. We do not speak here of the construction of roads to which our rulers have already turned their attention. We allude to measures which may be calculated to prevent such awful visitations as we are even now witnessing in Behar, as well as the still more serious evil in the shape of annual epidemics which have already devastated villages and districts. Famines must be prevented somehow,—and yet we do not know how they can be prevented except by an extensive system of irrigation for which the resources of the country are not equal. The attempt, however, may be made with advantage,—a portion of the vast sums of money now expended in useless barracks may be diverted to the construction of canals and irrigation works all over the country. The work will be slow no doubt, but year after year it will be seen to progress, and every new year will find us nearer our object than the preceding year.

But before entering into the question as to how famines may best be prevented in future, there is an important discussion which meets us at the very threshold. There are those who consider famines as one of the normal conditions of life in India, as a periodical and necessary check on the perpetual increase of a population with whom all prudential and rational restraints are unknown. There can be little doubt that, before the English came into this country, periodical wars, invasions and famines carried off, from time to time, large proportions of the ever increasing population of India. The English have blessed India with a long century of peace, they have afforded security of life and property to the meanest peasants, and they are contemplating measures for the prevention of famines in future. It is plausibly argued that all the various checks to the increase of population in India are one by one being removed, that food and the necessaries of life are imprudently promised to the poor, however recklessly they may multiply, that, as an inevitable consequence, India will soon be overpeopled, and the inhabitants will inevitably be reduced to the very brink of starvation, and in the end suffer from miseries which it will be beyond the power of the best intentioned Government to alleviate.

Those who argue in this way have very erroneously interpreted the Malthusian theory of population, or at least have grossly erred in applying it to India. We believe as thoroughly as any one in the theory of

Malthus that poverty and death shall inevitably operate as a check to the increase of a people with whom prudential checks are unknown, but we hold that in India this check appears in the shape of the hardships and deaths in ordinary years, and not in the astounding calamities in years of famine.

We hold that the chronic poverty and frequent deaths among the poor people in *ordinary years* serve as an insurmountable barrier to the undue increase of population, and indeed proportion such increase to the food-supply of the country, that famines only serve to make sudden and fearful gaps which are again filled up within a few years of prosperity, (without any lasting benefits resulting,) and roll back the current of population as it were only that the tide may come up to its usual limits with the greater vehemence in a few years. We hold that if famines were prevented for ever, and the same yield of crop were secured for all years, these sudden decreases and increases in population would be put a stop to, but the permanent never-failing checks, the deaths and poverty in ordinary years, would ever keep population within due bounds, and proportion its increase to the increase of the food-supply of the country.

We read in history of fearful depradations and inroads of predatory hordes which for years together depopulated large tracts of the country. Villages were deserted and cultivated fields relapsed into jungles. The waves of invasion however soon subsided into rest, the cultivation of old fields was resumed, and the inhabitants in the depopulated tracts soon multiplied and reached their permanent limits. We read that in 1760 a fearful famine swept away a third of the population of Bengal, and about a third of the cultivated area of land relapsed into jungle. Scarcely a generation or two passed however before the population again came up to its permanent limits, that is those limits within which it was kept by permanent and not occasional causes. Years of comparative prosperity followed the year of famine, large acres of land were reclaimed, there was a plentiful supply of food, and consequently more children survived than in ordinary years, and thus the permanent limits of population were soon reached.

Now let us consider what would have been the result if there had been no depopulation by invasions, no famine of 1760. There would have been no sudden decrease in population, and there would have been no sudden filling up of the gap. No prudential restraints are ever exerted in India in the way of foregoing marriage or preventing the birth of children in poverty, and so the only difference between years of prosperity and years of misery must be sought for in the number of children that survive. If we take 60 per cent to be the proportion of children who live to be men and women, we may suppose the rate increasing to 70 per cent in years of prosperity immediately following such a calamitous year as 1760. If, then, the calamity of

1760 had never occurred, there would have been in the first place no fearful amount of sufferings and death by starvation, and seecondly, during the years of prosperity succeeding 1760, the proportion of children that survived would have remained at 60 per cent, and not risen to 70 per cent.

This, then, is *all* that we need apprehend if famines are effectually prevented in future, *viz*, the few years of prosperity (owing to decreased population) succeeding famines would not be enjoyed, and the usual death-rate of children would not be decreased. The apprehension of over-population is a bugbear,—the permanent barriers will never be outstripped, for permanent checks in the shape of death and poverty in ordinary years are constantly at work, day after day, month after month, year after year.

We hope we shall not be mistaken. Heaven forbid we should ever speak lightly of these permanent checks, this chronic misery of the poor people. But we accept it with resignation as a substitute for more fearful calamities. It is with acute sorrow that the ryot's wife sees any of her children die of insufficient nourishment or diseases generated by poverty—but yet the bereaved mother looks on her surviving children and dries her tears, and accepts such visitation with resignation as one of the conditions of the life of poverty she leads. The philosopher too acknowledges in such bereavements a necessary penalty for improvident marriages and the begetting of children in poverty. But the astounding calamities and miseries accompanying famines, which lay entire families low and depopulate villages, leave the ryot no source of consolation, and afford the philosopher no ground for explanation.

We admit, population has vastly increased under the British rule,—but such is the case simply because the resources of the country have been developed in these times of peace, and food supply has been increased. The condition of the people has not deteriorated,—on the contrary it has improved in many respects,—and that single fact proves conclusively that the increase of population has not been greater than in due proportion to the increase of the food supply of the country. Population in Bengal will never, and can never, overstep this permanent limit,—and all apprehensions therefore, on the subject, are groundless.

We trust therefore we have heard for the last time the argument that to prevent future famines would be to remove the salutary checks that have always existed on the increase of population in India. We sincerely trust Government will feel no sort of hesitation in proceeding to its generous and philanthrophic work of devising and executing plans for the prevention of famines in India.

The only efficacious plan for the prevention of future famines that we can think of is irrigation. "But the surpassing value of irrigation in India," says Mr. Taylor in a paper read before the East Indian Association, "is to be found in the insurance it effects against the horrors of famine. * * * * Droughts have occurred in India so frequently that their occurrence before long in some part or other of the country is reasonably to be expected; and famine, as the certain effect of drought, *can be prevented by irrigation.* Here, then, is clearly one of the most important duties that can be placed before the Government of any State. The task is one that only the Government can undertake; for it is not merely to carry out projects which promise to be remunerative in the ordinary sense of the word, it is to extend irrigation wheresoever irrigation is possible, throughout the country. Till that is done, and the danger of famine has been guarded against to the fullest extent, the English in India may replace anarchy by peace, and may distribute equal justice, and remove ignorance; but it cannot be said that they fulfilled their whole duty by the people of the country."

Sir Arthur Cotton has proved to demonstration that every undertaking in the way of irrigation in India has been attended with an increase in rent and revenue which entirely covers the expenditure. Irrigation, therefore, cannot bring about pecuniary loss in the end. To go into details, the Godavery works were estimated to cost about a million sterling and irrigated 480,000 acres. The Krisna works cost about £300,000 and irrigated 200,000 acres. The Toombhadra works cost £1,500,000 and has "water sufficient to irrigate 400,000 acres."

The Orissa works cost "£1,250,000 and might have irrigated 350,000 acres. The Soane works already cost £750,000 and "ought to water 1,500,000 acres," and lastly the Ganges canal cost £2,500,000 and waters 1,000,000 acres.

The last work has been completed, and gives an average expenditure of £2½ per acre, or £1,600 per square mile. To irrigate the whole of the provinces under the Lieutenant-Governor of Bengal and Assam would cost something like four hundred millions sterling. In other words, if a million sterling were spent each year in irrigating Bengal (and that is more than can be spared for Bengal, considering the claims of other parts of India) the whole of Lower Bengal will be irrigated four centuries hence!

But this is not a representation of facts in their correct light. The whole of Bengal cannot be irrigated and need not be irrigated. There are places, too far from rivers, where irrigation would be too costly, and there are other places where the crops are too poor to make irrigation works worth their expenditure. On the other hand the most fertile spots are those which are most interspersed with rivers and streams and where therefore irrigation works would be the cheapest. Such spots should be selected to begin with. We think a portion of Bengal, say a tenth, might be selected whose annual produce is so exhuberant as to represent not a tenth, but fairly a fourth of the total annual produce of Bengal. If this portion were properly irrigated,—which according to our calculation might be done in forty years, a fourth of the crops of Bengal would be rendered safe and secure against the effects of drought. This, then, is a satisfactory result. Forty years hence we shall be safe and secure as regards at least a very considerable and perceptible proportion of the total produce of Bengal, and every succeeding year will find us farther and farther advanced in our security against famines.

Another and a far simpler measure might also be undertaken with advantage. It would entail on Government a very trifling annual expense to maintain granaries along the shores of the Ganges. To store these granaries with two million tons of rice in an ordinary year when the commonest sort of rice sells at Rs. 1-8 or Rs. 1-4 the maund, would not cost Government much more than a million stirling;—and with two millions in its store the Government could boldly meet the severest famine that can ever be expected to visit Bengal. When the worst comes to the worst, Government would only have to open its granaries, and two million tons of rice would plentifully feed over half the population of Bengal for the entire period of four or five months between the sowing and the reaping seasons.

The measure seems to be so simple that it is a wonder it was not adopted before. The expense of looking after these granaries after they have been once stored,—the expense of disposing of old rice and buying new, if such is necessary,—all this would amount to a very trifling sum. Seventeen millions stirling are spent year after year on the army for the defence of the country from external enemies, an outlay of one million *once*, and of some thousands probably after that, year after year, can never be considered too much by a humane Government for the protection of the country from the direst of internal visitations.

How to mitigate the effects of the annual epidemics seems to be a question more difficult of solution. The harrowing accounts that we receive year after year of whole villages being deserted are such as to call forth pity from the most unfeeling heart. Government is doing much for the relief of the people, dispensaries are established in the hearts of districts; but the axe has not yet been laid at the root of the tree. Medical opinion is yet divided as to the cause of such epidemics, and so long as medical opinion is not agreed, we can hardly expect Government to undertake any really earnest measure. The theory that the obstruction of the natural sub-soil drainage of this country by the construction of roads and rails has been productive of epidemics seems to us to be sound, and to have been well established by an array of facts. But our own opinion on the subject is not worth much, and we shall therefore leave the subject, recommending only that a fair trial at least may be given to this theory which seems to be so plausible on the face of it.

We shall here conclude. The peasantry of Bengal have already reaped some advantages under the English rule in India, and may expect to reap some more in future. To continue our figure, some maladies have been cured, more relief may be expected. But has any radical change in the constituion been brought about? Will the patient continue to feel relief if the hand of the doctor is removed? We have seen elsewhere that under the British rule the royt enjoys some freedom, and feels some sort of assurance. This is certainly an improvement, but is it of a radical nature,—will the freedom and assurance continue if the British power is withdrawn from the country? Our reader anticipates the dismal answer that we have to make. Legislation canot impart a spirit of freedom to a nation,—it can for a time help and support those who cannot help themselves,—it cannot impart to them the strength to help themselves. We have seen in the second chapter that the zemindari system, in its worst features is,—not the making of this or that ruler,—but the result of climatic influences and of the national character. It may be counteracted for a time,—it can never be done away with in this unfortunate country. It is a disheartening fact,—but none the less true that if British Power is withdrawn from the country, before fifty years have elapsed the peasantry will sink down once more into that complete and voiceless servitude from which they have risen!

And yet our rulers need not despond. If one man is happier for one day it is so much gained for the cause of mankind;—if the peasantry of Bengal are happier under British administration than they were or would be under other rulers,—that is so much gained for humanity,—that is a fact of which England may be deservedly proud.

THE END.

APPENDIX A.

The Past.

(Being Extracts from Bernier's Travels.)

We have seen in chapter IV, that the notorious insecurity of life and property under the Mahommedan rule prevented the Peasantry from ever bettering their condition or even acquiring habits of prudence, foresight and rational reflection. We have seen that at a time when the savings of to-day could not be enjoyed to-morrow, all abstinence was folly, all foresight useless, and that the ryots thereforo revenged their wrongs by never learning to save a penny. We have seen that the British Government by putting salutary checks on the conduct and power of the zemindars has already done much good, and has freed the peasantry from the galling *servitude*, (we use the word advisedly) of ages. And we have recommended that further and more definite checks may be laid on zemindari exactions, and that thereby the condition of the peasantry may be bettered.

There are those however,—numbering in their ranks some of the most influential writers and members of our community, who think otherwise. They think that

R

the relation between the peasantry and their master in olden times was satisfactory, and that the ryots of those days, being completely in the power of the zemindars, confided in them with affection, and were looked upon and treated with the tender care due to children. They maintain that the British Government, by placing checks on the conduct of the zemindars, have for the first time aroused ill feelings between the ryots and their hereditary masters,—and they advocate (we blush to write it) that such checks may be once more removed so that the same satisfactory relationship which existed in former times may once more obtain between zemindars and ryots.

To such advocates of zemindari supremacy we commend the following. If they can induce themselves to place any reliance on the testimony of a reflective and accurate traveller and eye-witness, they will find that the condition of the Peasantry and the poorer classes generally was not *entirely* satisfactory in those days,—that the English have not been *entirely* wrong in curbing the hereditary oppressors of the poor.

R. C. D.

"The persons thus put in possession of the land, whether as timariots, governors or farmers, have an authority almost absolute over the peasantry, and nearly as much over the artizans and merchants of the towns and villages within their district; and nothing can be imagined more cruel and oppressive than the manner in which it is exercised. There is no one before whom the injured peasant, artizan or tradesman can pour out his just complaints, no great lords, parliaments, or judges of presidial courts exist, as in France, to restrain the wickedness of those merciless oppressors, and the cadies or judges are not invested with sufficient power to redress the wrongs of these unhappy people. The sad abuse of the royal authority may not be felt in the same degree near capital cities such as Delhi and Agra, or in the vicinity of large towns or seaports, because in those places acts of gross injustice cannot easily be concealed from the court.

"This debasing state of slavery obstructs the progress of trade and influences the manners and mode of life of every individual. There can be little encouragement to engage in commercial pursuits, when the success with which they may be attended, instead of adding to the enjoyments of life, provokes the cupidity of a neighbouring tyrant possessing both power and inclination to deprive any man of the fruits of his industry. * * * * *

"We have seen how in India the gold and silver disappear in consequence of the tyranny of timariots, governors, and farmers,—a tyranny which even the monarch, if so disposed, has no means of controlling in provinces not contiguous to his capital,—a tyranny often so excessive as to deprive the peasant and artizan of the necessaries of life and leave them to die of misery and exhaustion,—a tyranny owing to which those wretched people either have no children at all or have them only to endure the agonies of starvation and to die at a tender age,—a tyranny, in fine, that drives the cultivator of the soil from his wretched home to some neighbouring state in hopes of finding milder treatment, or to the army, where he becomes the servant of a common horseman. As the ground is seldom tilled otherwise than by compulsion, and as no person is found willing and able to repair the ditches and canals for the conveyance of water, it happens that the whole country is badly cultivated, and a great part rendered unproductive from the want of irrigation. The houses too are left in a dilapidated condition, there being few people who will either build new ones or repair those which are tumbling down. The peasant cannot avoid asking himself this question: 'Why should I toil for a tyrant who may come to-morrow and lay his rapacious hands upon all I possess and value, wlthout leaving me, if such should be his humour, the means to drag on my miserable existence?'" * *

Bernier's Travels in the Mogul Empire.

APPENDIX B.

The Present.

(Being Extracts from the Banga Darsana.)

We make the following translations from a series of articles written in Bengali by Babu Bunkim Chunder Chatterjea, B. L., on the cultivators of Bengal. The long experience of Babu Bunkim Chunder in the executive service, his powers of close obervation and sustained thought and correct generalization, and his earnest regard for truth are so well known, that we do not make any apology for quoting the following. We may add that the sentiments contained in the following fairly represents the *general* impression on the subject among all executive officers that we have come across,—among all officers, namely, who live in the moffussil and see with their own eyes the real state of things. It is not a little curious that in strange disregard of truth, a different sort of opinion should be coined in the metropolis, and propagated by the Press, representing zemindars as the martyrs of the day !

R. C. D.

CHAPTER I.

General Improvement of the Country.

One often hears of the general improvement of our country in these days. Our country was retrogressing for so many ages,—under the English rule however we are becoming civilized,—our country is deriving many advantages.

Do you not see what these avdantages are? Behold the railway train doing a month's journey in a day, and mócking the power of ten million celestial horses. Behold the steam ship, sailing with her load of merchandize, even as a sportive swan, on the breast of the same mighty Gaṇges whose heaving surges carried away the celestial elephant, powerless before her mighty force. Has your father at Benares fallen dangerously ill this morning?—Electricity comes down from the skies and gives you the information,—by night you sit by his feet and tend him in his illness. That sort of disease could not perhaps have been cured in former times,—the doctor cures it now by means of the improved medical skill of later days. The same portion of land, which with its spacious buildings smiles even like the star-decked sky, was perhaps in former times the home of the tiger and the bear. Yonder, you see a spacious public road,—fifty years ago you would have broken your leg there by falling on the muddy slippery place, or would perhaps have been killed by robbers;—gas burns there now with the radiance of ten million moons. Constables are stationed for your protection, carriages wait to take you. Look at the spot where you are sitting, in place of coloured mats and rags you find, carpet, couch, chandelier, candelabra, marble, alabaster! Who can recount everything? If the Baboo who is now surveying the satellites of Neptune with his telescope had been born 50 years ago, he would have worshipped the God Neptune with rice, plantains, smoke and light. And as for my unworthy self,—who am sitting in the chair and have commenced writing essays on social subjects for the *Banga Darsana* on foolscap paper, a hundred years ago I would have taken my seat on the floor, and held up a torn almanac to my nose, and brought on a headache by investigations as to whether it is allowable to eat *lao* fruit on the ninth day of the moon! Is not our country deriving advantages? The country is mightily blessed,—raise a chorus of triumph for such blessings.

Amid this profusion of blessings I have one question to ask,—who is blessed? Yonder Hasim Shekh and Rama Kyborto are tilling the soil with blunt ploughshares toiling under the midday sun and in ankle-deep mud with bare head and bare feet;—have they been blessed? Their head aches in the heat of the month of Bhadra, they are dying of thirst, and are drinking mud rather than water to slake their thirst, they are dying of hunger, but cannot go home and eat, for it is the sowing season. In the evening they return and only partially satisfy their hunger with big reddish grains of rice on broken earthen plates, with salt and chillies as their only condiments. After that they will lie down beside the cowshed on ragged mats or on bare earth; they do not feel the sting of mosquitos. The next morning they will again wade through knee-deep mud and go to labor;—perhaps the zemindar or the mohajan will arrest them in the way for outstanding debts and keep them sitting; or perhaps at the very time of tilling the zemindar will take away the bits of land from their possession;—what then is left for them to do that year? Starvation, starvation of themselves, wife and children await before. Say, ye fashionable Baboos with the spectacles on your nose! in what way have they been benefited, what good have you with your education done them? And thou Englishman! who contemplatest changes in laws and enactments with a stroke of the pen in thy right hand, and with thy left art stroking thy sable flowing beard, say thou what good have Hasim Shekh and Rama Kyborto derived from thee?

I say none at all,--and such being the case I will not, I cannot join in the chorus of jubilation and trumph raised for the good of our country.

* * * * * * *

The income from the cultivation of land has increased in two ways. Firstly, cultivation has been extended, and secondly the price of the produce has risen. The produce of a begah of land which fetched 3 rupees before fetches 6 rupees now, and a fresh begah of waste land has been brought under cultivation which yields another sum of 6 rupees. 12 rupees are now obtained now in place of 3 rupees obtained in former times.

It is no exaggeration to maintain that since the Permanent Settlement, the agricultural income of the country has increased four-fold. Who gets this increase?

This increase is purely agricultural,—and agriculturists should get it; our readers will probably suppose and they do so, but such is not the fact. We shall shew who gets it.

A part goes to the imperial treasury. It is shewn in the Circular of the Board of Revenue for 1870-71, that the country which yielded a land income of Rs. 2,85,87,722 at the time of the Permanent Settlement now yields Rs. 3,50,41,248. Some will be inclined to ask how an income which has been permanently settled can increase. Mr. Schalch has explained the means by which the revenue has increased,—such as the settlement of Toufir lands, resumption of lakhiraj lands, settlement of alluvial accreations, increase of rent in lands held khas by Government, &c. Some will suppose that the increase from such sources cannot be very much in future, but Mr. Schalch has shewn that the income is still steadily increasing. Thus Government is getting an increase of 62½ lacs of Rupees from the increase of the agricultural wealth of the country.

A portion of this wealth goes into Government treasury in a variety of other ways. The income from opium sale is partly agricultural wealth, the income from customs is also partly agricultural wealth.

Mr. Schalch states that traders and Mahajauns have obtained a large portion of this increase of agricultural wealth. That they have done so, at least to some extent admits of no doubt. Agriculturists are increasing in number, and with them the profits of the Mahajan are increasing; and the profits of the traders who buy grain in the fields and dispose of it in markets, are no doubt derived from agricultural wealth. But Mr. Schalch is mistaken in supposing that the traders and Mahajans obtain the greater portion of the increase of agricultural wealth. Mr. Schalch is not singular in this mistake,—the *Economist* supports the same view. The *Indian Observer* has demolished the arguments of the *Economist* on this subject, but we need not enter into such discussions here.

The greater portion of the increase of agricultural wealth is obtained by the zemindar. Most of the agriculturists are tenants-at-will, and the zemindar can eject them at his pleasure, rights of possession are in many places only chimerical, the ryots have rights of possession by law,—but not as a fact. They have to give up lands as soon as the zemindar wishes it,—whether they have any rights or not. How many ryots are there who can quarrel with a zemindar and then live in his lands ? As a consequence he who promises the largest rent gets lands from the zemindar. Population we have said is increasing ; we cannot prove this,—but we may accept it as a fact. The rent of land will increase with the increase of population. Two ryots will in the present day ask for the same bit of land which was formerly possessed by one, and the zemindar will give it away to the highest bidder. Rama Kyborto, we may suppose, has a good piece of land, and he pays rent of one rupee per begah. Hasim Shekh asks for the same bit of land and offers a rupee and a half. The zemindar orders Rama to step out. Probably Rama has no right of possession and he goes out at once, or perhaps he has such rights, but what can he do. Who can quarrel with the aligator and then live in water ? He waives his rights and leaves the land, and the zemindar gets an increase of eight annas per bigah.

In this manner the rent of most lands has at different times and on different favorable occasions been increased since the Permanent Settlement. There is no necessity of having recourse to law, the rent of land has increased even as the price of vegetables in a bazar increases,—when there is an increase of customers. The increase has been appropriated by zemindars.

Many people will question the correctness of what we have said. They will point to law,—to fixed rates,—to the kindness and sense of justice of the zemindars. Law !—it is a luxury in which the rich alone can indulge, and fixed rates have been increased in the way shewn above. And as for the kindness and sense of justice of the zemiudar,—it is another name for self-seeking and selfishness. He turns the screw as long as the screw will turn,—and when the screw will turn no more, *then* his kindness comes into play.* By thus turning the screw the zemindars have appropriated the larger portion of the increase of agricultural income in Bengal. Rent rolls have increased three or four times since the Permanent Settlement in most places,—in some places it has increased ten times. There are few zemindaries in which it has not increased at all.

We have shewn that the increase of the agricultural income of the country is shared by the imperial treasury, the zemindars, the merchants, the mahajans. Does the agriculturist himself get it? Does he who produces the crops get it?

We do not say that he does not get anything at all,—but his share represents the atom of an atom. What he does get has not altered his condition,—to the present day he cannot live entirely by the produce of the land. What he gets therefore is not worth speaking of. He who is entitled to the wealth obtains it not,—he who produces crops by the sweat of his brow does not come in for a share in the profits!

We have shewn that the country has decidedly improved. Agriculture smiles in the land, and wealth is increasing. The king, the zemindar, the merchant, the mohajan, are scrambling for this wealth,—they are all benefited by it. The cultivator alone is not benefited! Nine hundred and ninety-nine people out of a thousand have not been benefited. Those who wish may raise a chorus of jubilation on such improvement,—I will not. I cannot raise a song of praise till I see these nine hundred and ninety-nine people benefited!—*Banga Darsana*, Bhadra, 1279.

---

* We must freely confess that all zemindars are not of this description. There are some who are really kind and just.

CHAPTER II.

The Zemindar.

* * * * * What the cultivator of Bengal produces from the soil is not much. Out of that he has to provide for the expenses of cultivation which are not insignificant. The price of the seed grain, the pay of laborers, provisions for cattle, such and other items have to be provided for, and what remains is seized upon by the mohajan. The cultivator has now to pay off at an interest of 50 per cent what he borrowed for his living during the rainy season. If he has borrowed two *bees* of dhan in Srabun he must pay back three *bees* in Pous. Little remains after paying this off, and out of that little the zemindar's dues must be paid. What remains is the smallest portion of the smallest fraction,—it is the husk of the husk, the moisture in the sugar-cane after the juice has been drained, the sap in the withered leaf. It may somehow support the ryot or it may not. Does that go to the ryot's hut ? Listen.

The ryot reaps the Amon dhan in the month of Pous and pays the portion of his rent due at Pous kist*. Some pay it off entirely, others only partially. The corn is heaped, thrashed and taken to the *Gola*, and in due time carried to the *Hat* for sale, and with the proceeds of the sale the ryot goes to the zeminder's Kachari in Choitra, the last month of the year, to pay off the balance of the whole year's rent. 5 Rupees, let us suppose, was due from Poran Mondul at the Pous *kist*, of which he could only pay four at the time. 3 Rupees, let us suppose, is due from him at the Chait kist,

* *Kist* means the several instalments by which the rent is paid.

and he has accordingly come to pay off the total due of 4 rupees. The Gomoshta after looking over his account says "a sum of 3 Rupees is due from you for Pous Kist." Poran Mondul protests loudly, cries *Dohai*, possibly produces the receipt of Pous Kist or possibly cannot do that. Possibly the Gomashta did not give him a receipt at the time, or possibly he had given him a receipt of 2 Rupees after receiving 4 Rupees.

Anyhow Poran Mondul cannot get the final receipt of the year now unless he acknowledges that the sum of Rs. 3 is due from him. It is likely enough that the Gomashta would change the 3 into 13 rupees and sue for that sum if Poran does not consent to part with the lesser amount. Poran Mondul acknowledges the sum of. 3 rupees to be due from him. Suppose 3 rupees is really due from him. The Gomashta then calculates tho interest due. Four annas to the Rupee is the usual rate in zemindari accounts,—no matter what the length or the intervening time may be, be it one month or 3 years., Poran pays Rs. 3-12. He further pays Rs. 3 due from him at the Choitra kist. Then comes the Gomashta's allowance for keeping accounts, the rate is 2 pice per rupee. Poran Mondul holds a jumma of the annual value of 32 rupees. He pays an allowance of one rupee. Then comes *Parbani* or festive allowances. Naeb, Gomashta, Tehsildar, Muharrar, Paik,—all come in for Parbani. A fixed total sum is to be raised from the village on this account, and every ryot gives his share. Poran Mondal has thus to pay 2 rupees extra.

We admit that it is not by the zemindar's consent that all this extortion takes place. He receives nothing out of this except the rent due and the interest, the remainder is appropriated by the Naeb and the Gomashta. Who is to blame? The zemindar keeps a Naeb at the same pay that he gives to a gate-keeper; the Gomashta's pay is somewhat less than that of a menial servant. How are they to support themselves unless they resort to such means? True, it is not by the zemindar's orders that all this extortion takes place,—but it is the result of his niggardliness. He feels no injury if his servants extort sums of money from the cultivators! Why should he interfere!

Then comes the *Punyaha* (festive day) of the new year in Ashar. Poran pays 2 rupees at the *Punyaha* kist, but that is the rent legally due,—he must pay something extra as present to the zemindar on that festive day. Perhaps there are several zemindars claiming shares in the same estate,—each receives *presents* separately. Then comes the Naeb for his *nuzzurs*,—that is paid. Then the Gomashtas claim their due!—they too are paid. The ryot whose stock is exhausted by these *nuzzurs* is unable to pay the rent due.—That will be recovered some other time.

Poran Mondul, let us suppose, pays everything, and returns home and finds he has nothing to live upon,—while the sowing season is approaching which must put him to some expense. He is not daunted. It is a thing that happens every year. He goes to his mohajan and borrows dhan at an interest of 50 per cent. He will pay off this debt again in the next year and be a beggar again. Cultivators always live on borrowed dhan,—always pay interest at 50 per cent. At this exorbitant rate kings may be turned beggars,—not to speak of cultivators. Sometimes the zemindar is himself the Mohajan and has *golahs* of dhan in the village, and Poran brings dhan thence. To drive on such a trade is certainly not unprofitable for the zemindar. He first extorts everything from the ryot and reduces him to beggary, and then lends him money at an interest of 50 per cent. The sooner the ryot is reduced to beggary the more is he the gainer.

It is not in every year that a good harvest is obtained. Excessive rain-fall, drought, rains out of season, inundation, locusts, any one of these causes may injure the crops. Mohajans lend dhan only when there is a prospect of a fair harvest, for they know very well that the agriculturists will not be able to pay off their debts if the harvest does not turn out fair. In unfavorable years the cultivator is left without any means of support, and starve with his family. Their only hope, then, is in having recourse to wild fruits and roots, or in relief, or in begging, or in God alone. With a few noble exceptions zemindars in such times do not help their ryots. Let us suppose it is a year favorable to good crops, Poran Mondul gets dhan from his Mohajan and so supports himself.

Then comes the Bhadra kist. Poran has nothing left and is unable to pay anything. Paik, Peon, Nagadi, Halshanas, Kotal or some other person bearing some similar name comes to takeed him. Perchance he is unable to get anything and returns without doing any harm, or perhaps Poran borrows the sum and pays off the sum due. Or perhaps Poran is foolish enough to quarrel with the peon. The peon returns to the Gomashta and says "Poran Mondul has called you *sala*." Three people are instantly sent to seize Poran, who drag him to the Kachari. There Poran has to put up with some bitter abuses, or receives perhaps some rough handling to boot. The Gomashta then fines him five times the amount due, plus the peon's fee, and orders his men to make Poran sit there till the amount is paid. If Poran has any friend he comes in and pays the fine and liberates Poran. Otherwise he remains confined in the Kachari one, two, three, five, seven days probably. Poran's mother or brother probably goes to Thana and lodges a complaint. The Sub-Inspector (in charge of the Thana) sends a constable to liberate Poran from confinement. The constable, who considers himself supreme in the realm, takes his seat in the Kachari with assumed importance and greatness. Poran cries a little, the constable shews off his authority, but has not a word to say about liberating the prisoner,—he is a paid servant of the zemindar,—gets *parbani* twice a year and as a matter of course can not do much. He receives something from the Gomashta, and in the gladness of his heart goes back and reports "there was no illegal confinement, Poran Mondul is a budmash and was concealed under a palm-tree near a pond and came up to me from that place saying he was confined." The case is dismissed.

It is not for arrears of rent only that ryots are taken to the Kachari, confined, beaten and fined. Anything induces the Gomashta to act thus. Gopal Mundul pays a present to the Gomashta and lodges a complaint "Poran will not eat with me." Poran is seized and brought to the Kachari. Nepal Mondul makes a similar present and complains "Poran has intrigue and intercourse with my sister." Poran Mondul is seized and brought to the Kachari. Information is received that Poran's brother's widow is with child. Poran is seized and brought to the Kachari. To-day Poran is unwilling to bear false witness for the zemindar. Poran is seized and brought to the Kachari.

Poran is at last let off, either because the Gomashta has recovered the fine imposed, or because Poran has offered security for the sum, or because Poran writes out a document acknowledging the debt, or because the Gomashta intends to recover the sum some other day, or fears some police officer might come in again, or perhaps thinking it useless to keep Poran confined any longer. Poran tills his land and sows dhan. The zemindar's daughter's daughter will be married in Agrahayana or perhaps it is the *anna prāsana* ceremony of his brother's child. Two thousand Rupees is fixed upon as the estimated expenditure. Each ryot must pay four annas to every rupee of rent payable. This will give five thousand rupees,—two thousand will be spent on the ceremony,—the remaining three thousand will find their way quietly into the zemindar's treasure vaults.

Those who can, pay the extra sum. Poran Mondul has nothing left,—he cannot pay. The full sum of five thousand rupees is not obtained from the zemindari. The zemindar resolves to visit his zemindari personally. The village is sanctified by his approach.

Now the Monduls of the village bring big black-colored goats to the Kachari as presents. Big live Ruhi, Katla, Mirigal and fish of other kinds lash their tails against the floor of the Kachari. Rooms are filled with large brinjals, potatoes, cauliflowers and peas. Curd-milk and milk, clarified butter and butter come in beyond measure. The ryots' love for their master is unlimited,—not so the digestive powers of the master. Even the paiks and peons, not to speak of the Baboo, begin to suffer from diarrhœa !

But all this is not to the point, the ryots must pay the "agomoni," the "nuzzar" and the "selami" since the zemindar has visited the village. A sum of 2 annas is again added to each rupee of rent due. But every one cannot pay so much. Those who can, pay it, those who cannot, are confined, or have the amount added to the rent due from them.

Poran Mondul cannot pay the amount, but his lands have produced good crops. The Gomashta sees this, and sends up a petition with an eight anna stamp affixed on it to the proper court for the assistance of the court in attaching Poran's property.

The substance of the petition is "the rent payable by Poran Mondul is in arrears, and we want therefore to attach his dhan. But Poran is a rioter, and has collected men to create disturbance and riot should we attempt to attach his dhan. Let a peon be sent by the Court to help us in attaching the dhan." The Gomasta is quite a harmless inoffensive man,—Poran alone is to blame for everything. A peon therefore is appointed by Court. The peon comes to the fields and receives money from the Gomoshta. Instead of attaching the dhan he has it all cut and stored in the zemindar's Kachari. This is called *krok Sahāyatā !*

Poran has lost everything. He cannot pay off the Mohajan's debts, or the zemindar's rent,—he has nothing to live upon. All this he has borne, for who can quarrel with the alligator and then live under water? But now Poran learns that he may lodge a complaint under such circumstances. Poran now means to lodge a complaint. But this is sooner said than done. Court House is even like gay house,—there is no entering without money. The value of stamp,—the vakeels' fees, fees for processes on witnesses and defendant, witnesses' expenses, remuneration of witnesses,—all these are necessary. Probably an Ameen's expenses must be paid down, the peons and amlahs of the Court expect something too. Poran has nothing left. He sells his plough and cattle and his utensils, and lodges complaint. He had done better if he had hanged himself.

Instantly a cross complaint is lodged on the side of the zemindar ;—Poran Mondal has disobeyed the order of attachment, and has cut and sold his dhan. The witnesses are all ryots of the zemindar,—all obedient to the zemindar for fear if not for love ; they all depose in favor of the zemindar. The peon who had been sent to help the attachment receives some further gratification, and deposes for the zemindar. Every one deposes that Poran has disobeyed the Court's order and cut and sold his dhan. The zemindar gets the decree, Poran's case is dismissed. Poran has now to make good the zemindar's damages, has to pay the zemindar's expenses in both the cases,—has to pay his own expenses in both the cases.

Poran has not a pice left, how is to pay all this ? If he can pay it by selling his land he does so,—otherwise he goes to jail, or leaves his home and country and absconds.

We do not say that all these acts of oppression are committed against any single ryot in any single year, or that every zemindar acts in this way. The country would have been laid waste if such were the case. Poran is an imaginary person,—we intended to describe all the oppressive acts of oppressive zemindars by naming one imaginary person. All these various acts are usually committed on various persons at various times.

Not that we can even hope to recount all the oppressive acts that are committed by zemindars. It is impossible to make a complete category of the various ways in which zemindars in various districts extort money from their ryots. The same rule does not prevail everywhere, all zemindars living in the same place do not follow the same method either, many have no method at all, but extort what sums of money they can, at any time and by any means.

As an instance we shall state a real occurrence and quote a list of sums which were actually extorted.

The occurrence took place in a village situated in the country which was inundated last year.* He who would know the name of the village may refer to the *Observer* of the 31st August last† page 131. The village appeared like an island in the midst of a sea. The crops of the villagers were all destroyed. Cattle died of starvation. The villagers became anxious for their lives. A zemindar in such times should have helped the ryots with money and provisions. If he had even remitted rent it would have done much good. Nay if he had only delayed the realization of the rent for some time, it would have been something. Far from it the Gomashtas now came with paks, peons and retainers to levy *illegal demands.* There were only some 12 or 14 khudkhast ryots and about as many laborers in the village. A list was made out, and a sum of Rs. 54-2 was to be levied from these people. We subjoin the list.

	Rs.	As.	P.
Nuzzer to the naeb on the festive day of the new year (Punyáha)	6	0	0
Ditto to Zemíndars (five co-sharers) ...	5	0	0
Ditto to Gomastas	2	0	0
Bamboo tolai of Gopalnaggur	1	0	0
Peon's talabana (fees) for Ashar kist ...	0	13	0
Ditto for Bhadra	1	5	0
Boat hire	1	8	0
Puja present to the Sudder Amla	6	8	0
Ditto to Jamadar of the Kachari	1	0	0
Caried over ...	25	2	0

* 1871. † 1872.

Brought forward	25	2	0
Puja present to Halshanas of the Kachari ...	1	0	0
Ditto to the five co-sharers (zemindars) ...	5	0	0
Ditto to Sriram Sen, Head Muharrar ...	1	0	0
Alms to the religious guide of the zemindars ...	2	0	0
Ditto to Gomashtas	12	0	0
Ditto to Muharrars	3	0	0
Parboni to the Barkandaz on the Dole festivity	1	0	0
Dak Tax	3	0	0
	54	2	0

Each ryot was to pay three annas to each rupee of rent due at this critical time of distress. It was impossible to realize the amount, but Gomashtas make impossible possible. The ryots worked, begged, sold their things, borrowed from others and paid off the amount. One would suppose oppression had been screwed up to the last point to which it could be borne,—but the Gomashtas did not suppose so. They seemed to think each ryot was a god of gold. Four or five days after the above sum had been realized they came in with a fresh demand of 40 rupees on account of the marriage of a girl of the zemindari family.

The ryots were helpless. They hired a boat and went to an indigo factory to borrow money. They were refused. They went to their mohajan to borrow money. They were again refused.

The ryots had then recourse to the last means left. They lodged complaint in the Magistrate's Court. The Magistrate convicted the defendants. They appealed. The jndge declared "It is true the ryots have been grievously oppressed, but I am bound by law to release defendants." This is justice! Every one knows justice consists in the release of prisoners!

This is no fable. We have extracted it from the *Indian Observer*. Bad men are to be found among all classes of people. To mention the acts of one or two bad men as a reflexion against the whole class would be unjust. If the above had been a solitary instance we would not have quoted it. It is not a solitary instance,—it is an occurrence which takes place frequently. He who denies this has no knowledge of our villages.

Let the reader look at the last item of the above list—"Dak Tax." Government is imposing a variety of taxes, and the zemindars loudly discuss the propriety of such impositions. But do they pay all such taxes themselves? This "Dak Tax" is an instance in point. Government has enacted that zemindars should pay for the carriage of letters in the mofussil. The zemindars say "well, we shall pay it if we are required to do so, but we shall not pay it out of our own pocket. We shall in our turn impose taxes on the ryots. And since we must impose it let us impose it somewhat heavily, so that there may be some profit left for us." And they do so. Mofussil letters are conveyed at the expense of the ryots, the zemindars come in for an extra profit. Government, when imposing new taxes, should consider who will pay them in the end.

It is the same with the Income Tax. The ryots pay for the zemindar, and the zemindar gets something as profit.

Those who take khas mehals have to pay for the "road fund." We have seen the "road fund" entered in the jumma wasil bawkee of the zemindar.

Government has not yet commenced levying "road cess,"* but zemindars have commenced levying the same. They

* This was written in October 1872.

have a right to levy it at the rate of a pice per rupee of rent payable. A certain zemindar in a certain district commenced levying the same at the rate of four annas per rupee. A ryot refused to pay it, and was dragged to the Kachari and maltreated. The ryot lodged a complaint, and the defendant was *not* released this time *by law*. The zemindar is in prison now.

But the most amusing thing of all is the following account of "*Hospitalee.*" Sub-divisional officers are ever ready to found schools and dispensaries. A certain Assistant Magistrate in District 24-Pergunnahs convened a meeting in his Sub-division to raise subscriptions for a dispensary. Every one promised contribution and went home. One of them passed an order "I shall have to pay so much per month in support of a hospital. Let each ryot pay one anna to the Rupee of rent payable as Hospitalee." The Gomashtas began to levy the amount, while on the other hand the dispensary was somehow never established. The zemindar had never to pay a pice in support of a dispensary for which ryots continued to pay at the rate of one anna to the Rupee. A few years passed on and the zemindar brought a suit against the ryots for increase of rent under Act X of 1859. The ryots said "we have been paying rent at a fixed rate since the Permanent Settlement, so that the rate admits of no increase according to law." The zemindar replied "there has been an increase of one anna per Rupee since such a year, and hence I am entitled to increase of rent."!

We have now a few words to say for the zemindars.

In the first place we have already stated before that all zemindars are not oppressive. The number of oppressive zemindars is decreasing day by day. The enlightened zemindars of Calcutta are not oppressive, and whatever oppression their ryots are subjected to takes place without their knowledge and against their will, and is caused by subordinate Naebs and Gomashtas. The same thing may be said of many enlightened zemindars in the mofussil. Big zemindars are not very oppressive,—some of them are not oppressive at all. It is the petty zemindars who are prone to oppressing. A zemindar receiving an annual rent of a lac of rupees does not feel the inclination to raise an additional sum of 25,000 rupees by unjust exactions; while he who scarcely gets 1,200 rupees in a twelve month, and yet must live in the style of a zemindar, necessarily feels inclined to raise something more by beating and extortion. Patnidars, Durpatnidars, and Ejaradars again are generally more oppressive than zemindars. For the sake of brevity we have, in the above article, used the word zemindar to imply every one who receives rent from ryots. The intermediate tenants receive an ejara or a putni talook with the object of keeping for themselves a clear profit after giving the zemindar his profit, so that they have to exact from the ryots an additional sum representing their profit. The creation of subordinate talooks is injurious to ryots.

Secondly.—The acts of oppression detailed above are often committed by Naebs and Gomashtas without the knowledge and against the will of the zemindars. Many zemindars are not aware that their ryots are oppressed at all.

Thirdly.—In many cases the ryots are to blame, and do not pay the rent due without oppression. The zemindari would be sold if every particular ryot were to be legally sued for rent. But we are bound to add in this connexion that *ryots never turn against their masters unless they are oppressed in the first instance.*† * * * * *

Banga Darsana, Kartick, 1279.

† The Italics are our own. We wish to draw particular attention to this fact the truth of which is undeniable.—R. C. D.

APPENDIX C.

THE FUTURE.

(Being Extracts from the Indian Mirror.)

THE following essays which we extract from the *Indian Mirror* are from the pen of Babu Jogesh Chunder Dutt. Though we do not agree with everything that has been said, yet the papers are thoughful and suggestive, and throw out practical hints on a subject of vital importance to the future welfare of the country.

R. C. D.

MANUFACTURE.

No doubt it is extremely gratifying to our vanity to say as has been said by some of our countrymen, that we are advancing in civilization with such rapid strides that we may ere-long hope to compete with the best civilized countries in Europe. But those who will not be deceived by the false colorings of vanity will find ample reasons to be grieved at the slow progress, if progress at all, we are making.

It may be pointed out with pride how some of our countrymen have attained renown in several branches of science and literature, how students in medicine, law, or mathematics in this country may be compared with advantage with their fellow-brethren of other countries, and how some have filled with honor and distinction responsible posts under the Government. But what are these in relation to civilization? Indeed what is civilization? We believe we are not far from the truth in stating that civilization consists in the conquests and triumphs of man over Nature and the powers and resources of Nature. No doubt a sound education and learned discoveries help us in making such conquests; but the true and only *index* of the civilization of any country is the extent to which nature has been subdued and brought under the control of man,—in other words, the extent to which arts and manufactures have been developed. Tested by this standard, what is our civilization worth? How far have we learnt to bring Nature under our control, and make her conducive to our own interests, comforts and conveniences? Are not our villages and huts built on the same plan and principle, and do not our villagers content themselves with the same scanty conveniences of life as before the Mahomedan conquest? Are not our implements of agriculture as simple as heretofore? True, the conveniences of city life have much improved, but should we thank ourselves for that? The clothes we wear are not of our manufacture, the industry of our people has not produced the paper or the steel pen with which we write. Have our arts and manufactures improved? If not, our boasted education is but a vain show, and science among us is reduced to the level of idle romance.

If we look back to history we find that the civilization of a country is always in proportion to the state of her arts and manufactures. England, France and America are in the present day considered to be the most civilized countries in the world, and it is precisely in these countries that arts and manufactures are best flourishing. The civilization of Holland declined from the time when her weavers and artists left her shores for England, and the civilization of Russia began when Peter the Great introduced into that country foreign arts and manufactures. In the face of such facts it requires no little hardihood to assume that progress in civilization is possible without due attention being paid to arts and manufactures. And now let us enquire what we have learnt within the last hundred years of our boasted progress in civilization.

It is indeed humiliating to reflect on the backward condition of our arts and manufactures. India is a rich country in her natural products; what a vast quantity of raw materials is being exported year after year! Cotton, Jute, Silk and various other products are being continually carried out that they may be turned into articles useful to man by the skill and industry of other people. If we had only known to utilize these materials here, what a vast amount of wealth would have been secured to us. Numbers of our people might have been profitably employed, population would have increased, wealth would have increased, civilization would have progressed.—All these are now lost to us.

There was a time when India was famous for her manufactories, and suplied nations of the far west with her manufactured articles. The Bazars of Damascas and Bagdad, the shops of Alexandria, the markets of Venice and Genoa were stored with Indian goods; and Indian silk brocades, Indian pearls, Indian ivory works and Indian muslins were sought for, by the Kalifs, the Emperors, and the Doges. India has now forgotten to manufacture articles for her own children. Western nations have with the aid of science substituted steam for handiwork, and as we could not follow up the improvements and discoveries, we have no other alternative than to depend on the western nations for almost every article of utility or luxury.

Never perhaps in the annals of India were greater facilities afforded to us to civilize ourselves than at the present day. The continual series of wars and devastations, of oppressions and rebellions, of rise and subversion of empires and kingdoms, which disfigure the Mahomedan period of our history, left little opportunity to the people to think of science, arts, or manufactures. Every tribe was armed to the teeth, and was fighting with its neighbours without interruption, and his best energies were employed in protecting its own against the ever-invading foe. That was a period of deadly struggle for existence. Now under the British rule peace has been restored to the country, and we have leisure to look round us. A flood of the light of western civilization, too, is being poured into our country, calculated to make us educated and reflective beings. We may calmly reflect on the means of the advancing civilization of Europe, and we may make an attempt to adopt similar means; we may travel to Europe to learn those arts and manufactures, and import them home. This, it must be admitted, is a comparatively easy mode for a people to become civilized, for we have only to pluck the fruits, as it were, which have been grown in Europe after years of perseverence, patience and thought; and if we are not prepared to undergo even this small trouble, we have good reasons to fear that we shall never be a nation worth existing.

Should we ask our Government to teach us arts and manufactures? The English, it should be acknowledged with gratitude, are educating us in science and literature, and are sparing no pains to make us civilized and happy; but to educate and enlighten us in this way *costs* our rulers nothing; educating us in manufactures and arts, educating us to utilize the natural products of India would probably interfere with their commercial interests and provoke the jealousy of a commercial people. The English, though just and generous, have a keen eye on their pecuniary interests and our request to be educated in arts would probably be made in vain. But there is a stronger ground why such a request should not be made. On principle we should ask no help from our rulers in this matter, we should much like to see our trades and manufactures improving by our own efforts and not by the assistance of our rulers. It is therefore with pleasure that we learn that a lucifer match manufactory and an iron manufactory have been established at Bombay, and also several Spinning and Weaving Mills both at Madras and Bombay with success; and that it is also proposed to establish a soap manufactory at Sholapore. We are also gratified to hear that very recently two of our countrymen proceeded to England with an expressed intention of learning English manufactories. Still such examples are comparatively very rare.

Indian Mirror, 17th October 1873.

Agriculture.

We have often heard our young men complain, in a somewhat melancholy tone, of the difficulty of getting a decent livelihood at the present day. Times are altered, they say with all the eloquence of disappointed hope, and B.A.s and M.A.s can hardly secure an employment of Rs. 40 or 50 a month. College graduates, they continue, have become as numerous as the pebbles in the streets, and every profession is over-stocked. There is some truth to be sure in their statement, but we ought rather to rejoice than lament that such a state of society is being daily developed in our country. If there are as many graduates as there are stones in the streets, it only shows the extent to which education has spread among our countrymen. Some professions have consequently been over-stocked, but has this over-stocking produced no good result? It is because we have more pleaders and sub-assistant surgeons than we require, that our young men have felt the necessity and inclination to turn out barristers and assistant surgeons. If there had been a chance of getting a good situation for every intelligent and educated young man here, we would perhaps never have seen so many of our countrymen aspiring after the civil service. It is because the profession is over-stocked here that our young men are gradually enlarging the scope of their ambition.

Let us on the other hand examine if all the professions are over-stocked, and if really there is nothing which an educated Bengali can follow with the certain hope of making pecuniary gain. We are sure that so far as law, medicine, engineering and Government service are concerned, they are pretty full; but it is hardly logical, therefore, to conclude that the difficulty of obtaining a decent means of livelihood has increased among us to an uncommon extent. The doors are yet open if our young men will only take the pains to walk in.

Of the numerous branches of industry to which our educated men are as yet strangers, agriculture is assuredly one. Bengal is one of the greatest agricultural districts in the world, and her rich alluvial soil, if properly cultivated, will produce gold, if we are allowed the expression; yet how neglected is our agriculture! It is entrusted to a poor half-starved peasantry, ignorant and oppressed. We are not aware of a single really educated Bengali who has taken to agriculture as a means of his livelihood, nor do we know of a single corn-field that is cultivated under his superintendence.

Accustomed to associate agriculture with the poor, half-fed and oppressed cultivators, our so-called gentry have come to look down on it as beneath their dignity. Many will gladly accept a service on a poor pittance of Rs. 40 or 50 a month rather than take to agriculture. It is to be hoped that education will do away with this, as it has done with many others of our prejudices, and that it will come to be considered, as really it is, a very healthy, pleasant and honorable calling. The advantages which our country may derive if her educated sons will follow this new path, can scarcely be overestimated.

In the first place we must have a set of educated farmers who will be able to bring the help of science to agriculture. Educated farmers may try experiments, may improve the land by proper manure and drainage, may use improved implements of tillage, and introduce other improvements by which they may cheapen labor and make earth more productive. Wonders have been achieved in England within the last century in agriculture, and by the help of arts and science even that barren island is forced to smile with the luxuriance of vegetation. Every nook and corner is taken advantage of, and made to yield to the comforts of man. What may not then be done if the same science were employed in the fertile lands of Bengal, and who can effectively employ it but her educated sons?

Secondly, the cultivation of our country under an educated agency may do much to avert the awful famines that not unfrequently visit us, leaving thousands and thousands dead, and many more in absolute poverty and acute distress. Want of rain may be compensated by artificial irrigation, and by other improvements, which education alone can suggest, we may be saved to a great extent from their ravages.

Thirdly, when a large portion of the educated people will have spread themselves in the interior of the country, settling here and there, and dotting the vast tract of Lower Bengal with their neat factories and farm-houses, they will naturally carry with them the civilization of the cities into the heart of the villages; and ignorant people coming in contact with them, their mode of thinking, their habit of living, their manner of operations, and their ever improving implements of husbandry, will no doubt imbibe much of the civilized ideas, and hankering after improvement which they now stand so much in need of. This in our humble opinion will be of greater service to the ignorant millions than what has hitherto been done to raise their much pitiable condition.

Fourthly, though neither the last nor the least of the benefits likely to raise from this system, is the reduction to its minimum of the oppressions practised upon our ignorant peasantry. Young Bengal cultivating large tracts of country will be too powerful either for the Zemindar or the police. In them will be found an effective protection to the people with whose interests theirs will be interwoven.

We have attempted to show some of the advantages our country may reap if our educated men will take to agriculture. But man is selfish and a Bengali is no exception to the rule. Mere love of patriotism will not induce him to undertake this vast enterprise, if it is not shown that every individual embarking on it has a fair chance of gain before him.

Those who are acquainted with the inner life of our peasantry will be able to say how much a peasant generally gains every year, and how he would soon mend his condition, were he not sometimes obliged to pay a ruinous interest for the money he borrows, and sometimes to bribe as heavily the men he dreads to keep himself safe from harm. These and items like these swallow up all his gain and leave him as much a beggar after as before the harvest. From such expenses an educated farmer, conducting his own farm with his own money, is necessarily free, and none will be able to wring a piece from him in an illegal way and under his direct supervision, and by the help of science, his gain, it can easily be conceived, will be immense. At any rate it will be far more paying, and far more pleasant than the ordinary service for which we appear so much anxious.

The condition of the present cultivators also will be much improved. They will find advantageous employment under their educated neighbours, and safe under their protection, as we have said before, they may escape the oppressions of the police and the zemindars for whom they never are an equal match.

Indian Mirror, *6th March* 1874.

Printed by I. C. Bose & Co., Stanhope Press, 249, Bow-Bazar Street,—Calcutta.